O Allah, send prayers upon our master Muhammad, the opener of what was closed, and the seal of what had preceded, the helper of the truth by the Truth, and the guide to Your straight path. May Allah send prayers upon his Family according to his grandeur and magnificent rank.

-SALĀT AL-FĀTIḤ

Title: The Honored One: Allah's Praise of His Beloved ﷺ

ISBN: 978-1-952306-23-5

FIRST EDITION | JANUARY 2024

AUTHOR: QĀḌI ʿIYĀḌ B. MŪSĀ AL-YAḤṢUBĪ
TRANSLATOR: JODY MCINTYRE
PROOFREADING: WORDSMITHS
TYPESETTING: IGP CONSULTING | WWW.IGPCONSULTING.COM
DISTRIBUTION: WWW.SATTAURPUBLISHING.COM

WWW.IMAMGHAZALI.CO

The Honored One

Allah's Praise of His Beloved ﷺ

Qāḍi ʿIyāḍ b. Mūsā al-Yaḥṣubī

محمد

صلى الله عليه وسلم

Contents

PUBLISHER'S MESSAGE VII

QĀḌI ʿIYĀḌ B. MŪSĀ AL-YAḤṢUBĪ XI

THE HONORED ONE: ALLAH'S PRAISE OF HIS BELOVED ﷺ

THE GLORIFICATION AND HONOURING OF THE MOST HIGH FOR HIS PROPHET ﷺ, THE CHOSEN ONE, THROUGH WORDS AND ACTIONS 2

ALLAH EXALTED PRAISING THE PROPHET ﷺ, AND HIS HIGH REGARD FOR HIM 6

ALLAH EXALTED DESCRIBING THE PROPHET ﷺ AS "A WITNESS", AND THE PRAISE AND HONOUR THAT IMPLIES 30

THE KINDNESS OF ALLAH WHEN HE ADDRESSES THE PROPHET ﷺ 40

ALLAH EXALTED SWEARING BY THE PRESTIGE AND HONOUR OF THE PROPHET ﷺ 48

ALLAH EXALTED TAKES AN OATH TO CONFIRM THE STATION OF THE PROPHET ﷺ WITH HIM: 56

ALLAH EXALTED ADDRESSING THE PROPHET ﷺ WITH AFFECTION AND GENEROSITY 72

THE NOBLE STATUS OF MUHAMMAD ﷺ AMONG THE PROPHETS 78

ALLAH EXALTED INSTRUCTING HIS CREATION TO SEND PRAYERS UPON THE PROPHET ﷺ, HIS PROTECTION OF THE PROPHET ﷺ, AND HIS REMOVAL OF PUNISHMENT BECAUSE OF HIM 86

Publisher's Message

All praise is due to Allah, the First; without a beginning, and the Last; without an end. Peace and prayers be upon the Prophet Muhammad ﷺ, the first Prophet on the Day of Judgement to offer intercession despite being the last Prophet sent, and upon his pure family, his blessed Companions, and all who follow their way upon the path of righteousness, until the day intercession begins with none other than the Prophet Muhammad ﷺ.

Al-Shifā bi Taʿrīf Ḥuqūq al-Muṣṭafā, directly translated as, 'The Remedy (or Cure) Through Recognizing the Rights of the Chosen One', is one of the most celebrated works in the genre of Shamāʾil. It stands uniquely amongst the works of Qāḍī ʿIyāḍ as his most celebrated effort–with many surviving manuscripts and commentaries found throughout the Islamic world. Shamāʾil is a genre of works that deals with the life, characteristics, and descriptions of the Prophet ﷺ and his station. There are many works in this genre, the most celebrated of which is *al-Shamāʾil al-Muḥammadiyyah*, which Imam Ghazali Publishing recently translated and published. Other works include commentaries and summaries of that nature, or hagiographical poems that recount the biography of the Prophet ﷺ and render praise to the Prophetic station.

However, *al-Shifā*, as it is called for short, stands alone as perhaps the most thorough work in this genre, dealing with both the descriptions of the Prophet ﷺ, his station and his perfections, and with the rulings pertaining to one's belief and treatment of him ﷺ. It is exhaustive in its treatment of the subject, expounding on topics that range from Allah's praise of the Prophet ﷺ and his status and station before Him, to the obligation of loving him and what that entails. In short, the uniqueness of this work can be attributed to its holistic coverage of the Messenger ﷺ. Historically, this work took on a form of sacredness and was revered throughout the Muslim world. With that in mind, the Qāḍī's intention for this blessed work was more so to address, what he understood as, a real and practical need in his society. In today's context, it is our intention to continue the spirit of his desire outlined for us in his introduction:

> You have repeatedly asked me to write something which gathers together all that is necessary to acquaint the reader with the true stature of the Prophet, peace and blessings be upon him, with the esteem and respect which is due to him, and with the verdict regarding anyone who does not fulfill what his stature demands or who attempts to denigrate his supreme status—even by as much as a nail-paring. I have been asked to compile what our forebears and imams have said on this subject, and I will amplify it with *ayāt* from the Qur'an and other examples...Writing about this calls for the evaluation of the primary sources, examination of secondary sources, and investigation of the depths and details of the science of what is necessary for the Prophet, what should be attributed to him, and what is forbidden or permissible in respect of him; and deep knowledge of Messenger-ship and Prophethood and of the love, intimate friendship and the special qualities of the sublime rank.[1]

---

1 Iyad ibn Musa, *Muhammad: Messenger of Allah: Ash-Shifā by Qadi 'Iyad* , translated by Aisha Abdarrahman Bewley, vi.

Although it has previously been translated into English in its entirety, our intention with this series is to attempt to bring out, for our readers, some of the most relevant smaller, yet critically important, topics related to the Prophet ﷺ, his station, our duty towards him, and the benefit of loving him and fulfilling our duty towards him. Such a task has been made easier for us by the expert arrangement of the text in terms of its sections and subsections. Each larger section is divided into smaller subsections, which facilitates targeted publications that are small but great in benefit. It is our desire, with having isolated smaller and somewhat easier 'quick-reads', as they are called, that readers may be inspired to complete a full reading of the noble Qāḍī's entire work.

TALUT DAWOOD
IMAM GHAZALI PUBLISHING

—

Qāḍi 'Iyāḍ b. Mūsā al-Yaḥṣubī

The Imām, the unique Ḥāfiẓ, Shaykh al-Islām, 'Allāmah, Qāḍi Abū al-Faḍl 'Iyāḍ b. Mūsā b. 'Iyāḍ b. 'Umar b. Mūsā b. 'Iyāḍ al-Yaḥṣubī al-Andalūsi al-Sibti al-Māliki was born in the year 476/1083–84, six months after the Almoravid takeover of the city. His ancestors left Andalus for Fez and then settled in Ceuta. At the age of 22, Qāḍi 'Iyāḍ obtained a license (*ijāzah*) from Ḥāfiẓ Abū 'Alī al-Ghasāni.

He left Ceuta on two occasions, one of which was to travel to Andalus (Spain) seeking out scholars with whom he could take knowledge. Between 507/1113 and 508/1114 the Qāḍi visited Cordoba, Almeria, Murcia, and Granada. During this time, he learned Ḥadith from the famed scholar, Qāḍi Abū 'Alī b. Sukrah al-Sadafi. Qāḍi 'Iyāḍ stayed with him closely. He also took Ḥadīth from Abū Baḥr b. al-'Ās, Muḥammad b. Ḥamdayn, Abū al-Ḥusayn Sirāj al-Saghīr, Abū Muḥammad b. 'Attab, Hishām b. Aḥmad and many other scholars. He learned jurisprudence (*fiqh*) from Abū 'Abdullah Muḥammad b. 'Isa al-Tamīmī and Qāḍi Muḥammad b. 'Abdullāh al-Masili.

The Qāḍi was first appointed judge of Ceuta in 515/1121 and served in his position until 531/1136. He would later serve again in Cueta from 539–543/1145–48. His tenure as a judge in Cueta was probably his most productive period; his casework created the foundations for his works in jurisprudence (*fiqh*). Khalaf b. Shakwal said of him:

> He is among the people of knowledge and polymaths, of great intelligence and understanding. He performed the duties of a judge in Ceuta for a long time, in which he earned a praiseworthy reputation. Then he travelled from there for a judgeship in Granada. However, he did not stay there long. Thereafter, he came to us in Cordoba and we took from him.

The jurist (*faqīh*) Muḥammad b. Ḥammadah al-Sibti said:

> The Qāḍi began training at the age of twenty-eight years and assumed judgeship at the age of thirty-five. He was lenient, but not weak, [and] fierce in defence of the truth. He learned jurisprudence (*fiqh*) from Abū 'Abdullah al-Tamīmī and accompanied Abū Isḥāq b. Ja'far. No one in Ceuta wrote more works than him during his time. He wrote the book 'Al-Shifā' fi Sharāf al-Mustafa', 'Tartīb al-Madārik wa Taqrīb al-Masālik fī Dhikr Fuqahā' Madhab Mālik', a multi-volume work, 'Kitāb al-'Aqīdah', 'Kitāb Sharḥ Ḥadīth Umm Zar'', the book 'Jāmi' al-Tārīkh' and others.

Many scholars narrate from Qāḍi 'Iyāḍ. Among them are Imām 'Abdullah b. Muḥammad al-'Ashīri, Abū Ja'far b. al-Qasir al-Gharnāti, al-Ḥāfiẓ Khalaf b. Bashakwal, Abū Muḥammad b. 'Ubayd Allah al-Hijri, Muḥammad b. al-Ḥasan al-Jābirī and his son, Qāḍi Muḥammad b. 'Iyāḍ, the Qāḍi of Denia (in Spain). Qāḍi b. Khalkhan said, 'The teachers of Qāḍi 'Iyāḍ number around one hundred. He passed away during Ramaḍan 544/December-January 1149–50.' Conversely, it has also been reported that he died in Jumada al-Ākhirah of the same year, in Marrakesh. His son passed away in the year 575 AH.

Ibn Bashakwal said, 'Qāḍi 'Iyāḍ passed away to the west of his hometown, in the middle of the year 544 AH." His son, Qāḍi

Muḥammad, said, 'He passed away in the middle of the night, on Friday 9 Jumada al-Ākhirah. He was buried in Marrakesh in the year 544 AH.'

al-Dhahabī said, 'it has reached me that he was killed by an arrow for his denial that Ibn Tumart was infallible'.

Some of the Qāḍi's well-known works are:

1. Al-Shifā' bi Ta'rīf Ḥuqūq al-Mustafā – the Shifa' remains one of the most commentated books of Islām.
2. Tartīb al-Madārik wa Taqrīb al-Masālik li Ma'rifat A'lām Madhab Mālik.
3. Ikmāl al-Mu'lim bi Fawa'id Muslim – Qāḍi 'Iyāḍ's own commentary was expounded upon heavily by Imām al-Nawawi in his commentary of Saḥiḥ Muslim.
4. Al-I'lām bi Ḥudūd Qawā'id al-Islām – a work on the five pillars of Islām.
5. Al-Ilma' ilā Ma'rifa Usūl al-Riwāyah wa Taqyīd al-Sama' – a detailed work on the science of Ḥadīth.
6. Mashāriq al-Anwār 'ala Saḥiḥ al-Athar – a work based on the Muwaṭā of Imām Mālik, Saḥiḥ Al-Bukhāri of Imām Bukhāri, and Saḥiḥ Muslim by Imām Muslim.
7. Al-Tanbihāt al-Mustanbaṭah 'ala al-Kutub al-Mudawwanah wa al-Mukhtalaṭah.
8. Daqā'iq al-Akhbar fi Dhikr al-Jannah wa al-Nār – a work describing the joys of Heaven (*Jannah*) and the horrors of Hell (*Jahannam*).

The Honored One
Allah's Praise of His Beloved ﷺ

Qāḍi ʿIyāḍ b. Mūsā al-Yaḥṣubī

The Glorification & Honouring of the Most High For His Prophet ﷺ, The Chosen One, Through Words And Actions

Any person who has had any engagement with the topic at hand, or possesses the slightest degree of understanding, will be aware of the great esteem in which Allah Exalted holds our Prophet ﷺ. He singled him out for virtues and qualities too numerous to quantify, and any attempt to do so would exhaust tongues and pens.

We can glimpse the honouring of the Almighty for His Prophet ﷺ from that which is stated in His Book, that which He informs us of his elevated positions, and that which He praises of his character. He encourages His slaves to hold tight to the way of the Prophet ﷺ and to join him in obeying His Commands. Allah ﷻ is the One who favoured His Prophet ﷺ [above all creation], then purified him, then praised him on account of that, and finally rewarded him with the greatest reward. To Him belongs Grace in beginning and returning, and to Him belongs Praise and Gratitude in this world and the next.

He presented His Prophet ﷺ to His creation in the most complete and perfect form, and distinguished him with beautiful characteristics and a praiseworthy manner. He had a noble way and was blessed with innumerable virtues. Furthermore, Allah Exalted supported him with the ability to perform astounding miracles and deliver irrefutable signs. These were witnessed by his contemporaries and Companions and their knowledge was passed down to those who came after them, until the understanding of this reality reached us and we were overwhelmed with his light. May the abundant praise

فِي تَعْظِيمِ الْعَلِيِّ الأَعْلَىٰ لِقَدْرِ [هذا] النَّبِيِّ المُصْطَفَى قَوْلاً وَفِعْلاً

قال الفقيه القاضي الإمام أبو الفَضل رحمهُ اللهُ:

لا خفاء على مَنْ مارس شَيْئاً من العِلْم، أو خُصَّ بأدْنَى لمحة[١] مِنْ فَهم، بتعظيم الله تعالى قَدْرَ نبينا عليه [الصلاة والسلام]، وخصوصِه إياه بفضائل ومحاسن ومناقبَ لا تنضبط لزمام، وتنويهه[٢] مِنْ عظِيم قَدْرِه بما تَكِلُّ[٣] عنه الألسِنةُ والأقلام. **فمنها**: ما صَرَّح به تعالى في كتابه، ونَبَّه به على جَليل نصابه[٤]، وأثنى به[٥] عليه من أَخلاقه وآدابه، وحضَّ العبادَ على التزامِه، وتَقلُّدِ إيجابه[٦]؛ فكانَ - جلَّ جلالُه - هو الذي تفضّل وأَوْلىٰ، ثم طَهَّر وزَكَّى، ثم مَدَحَ بذلك وأثنىٰ، ثم أَثاب عليه الجزاءَ الأَوْفَى، فله الفَضْلُ بَدْءاً وعَوْداً، وله الحمد أُولىٰ وأُخرىٰ. **ومنها**: ما أَبْرَزَه للعِيان مِنْ خَلْقِهِ على أتمِّ وجوهِ الكمال والجلال، وَتَخصِيْصِهِ بالمحاسن الجميلة، والأخلاق الحميدة، والمذاهب الكريمة، والفضائل العديدة؛ وتأييدِهِ

---

(١) أدنى لمحة: أقل قدرٍ.

(٢) تنويهه: إشادته ومدحه. ومن الخطأ الشائع استعمال (نوّه) بمعنى (أشار)

(٣) تَكِلُّ: تعجز وتعيىٰ.

(٤) (جليل نصابه): أي: عظيم منصبه وشرفه ورفعته.

(٥) «به»، لم ترد في المطبوع

(٦) (تقلد إيجابه): أي بإطاعة جنابه فيما أوجبه في كتابه/ قاله القاري ١/٦٩.

and salutations of Allah be upon our Prophet ﷺ.

I read the following hadith to the esteemed scholar Abū ʿAlī (the great *ḥāfiẓ* al-Ḥusayn ibn Muhammad [al-Ṣadafī]), who said: "It was narrated from Abū al-Ḥusayn, from al-Mubārak ʿAbd al-Jabbār and Abū al-Faḍl Aḥmad ibn Khayrūn, who both narrated from Abū Yaʿlā al-Baghdādī, from Abū ʿAlī al-Sinjī, from Muhammad ibn Aḥmad ibn Maḥbūb, from Abū ʿĪsā al-Ḥāfiẓ[1], from Isḥāq ibn Manṣūr, from ʿAbd al-Razzāq, from Maʿmar, from Qatādah, from Anas, [who said] that al-Burāq was brought to the Prophet ﷺ on the night of al-Isrā'[2], saddled and reined, but shied away from him. Jibrīl said to al-Burāq: 'Do you act like this with Muhammad? You will never have a rider more honoured by Allah Exalted than him!' Anas added: 'Al-Burāq began to sweat profusely.'"[3]

1 Better known as Tirmidhī.

2 Al-Isrā' wa al-Miʿrāj: the miraculous Night Journey.

3 Reported here from the chain of Tirmidhī (3131). Also reported by Aḥmad (3/164), Abū Yaʿlā (3184), and others. Authenticated by Ibn Ḥibbān in *Al-Iḥsān* (46). Tirmidhī said: "This hadith is *ḥasan gharīb*."

بالمعجزات الباهرة، والبراهين الواضحة، والكرامات البيّنَة التي شَاهَدَها مَنْ عاصَره، ورآها من أَدْركه، وعَلِمَهَا عِلْمَ يَقِين من جاءَ بعده، حتى انتهى عِلمُ حقيقة ذلك إلينا، وفاضتْ أنواره علينا، ﷺ كثيراً. حدثنا القاضي الشهيد أبو علي: الحُسين بن محمد الحافظ - رحمه الله - قراءةً مِنّي عليه؛ قال: حدثنا[٧] أبو الحسين: المبَارك بن عبد الجبَّار، وأبو الفَضْل: أحمد بن خَيْرُون (٤/أ)؛ قالا حدَّثنا أبو يَعْلى البغدادي؛ قال: حدثنا أبو علي السِّنْجِي؛ قال: حدثنا محمد بن أحمد بن محبوب، [قال]: حدثنا أَبو عِيسى بنُ سَوْرَةَ الحافظ؛ قال: حدثنا إسحاق بن منصور، حدثنا عبد الرزَّاق، أخبرنا مَعْمَر، عن قَتَادَةَ، عن أَنَسٍ، أن النبي ﷺ أُتي بالبُرَاق ليلَةَ أُسْرِي به، مُلْجَماً مُسْرَجاً، فاستَصْعَبَ عليه؛ فقال له جبريلُ: أَبِمُحَمَّدٍ تَفْعلُ هذا؟ فما رَكِبَكَ أحدٌ أكرمُ على الله تعالى منه. قال: فارْفَضَّ عَرَقاً.

---

(٧) كلمة «حدثنا»، لم ترد في المطبوع

Allah Exalted Praising The Prophet ﷺ, & His High Regard For Him

Know that the Book of Allah contains many verses which mention the Prophet ﷺ in a beautiful way, enumerate his qualities and virtues, and glorify his status. We have relied here on those verses most apparent in meaning.

Allah Exalted praises the Prophet ﷺ abundantly and repeatedly mentions his qualities. He says: "There certainly has come to you a messenger from among yourselves ['*min anfusikum*']. He is concerned by your suffering, anxious for your well-being, and gracious and merciful to the believers."[4] Al-Samarqandī[5] said: "[In the above verse] some recited '*min anfasikum*'[6], with a *fatḥah* on the *fā*, although the majority read '*min afusikum*'[7], with a *ḍammah* on the *fā*.

Allah Exalted taught the believers, or the Arabs, or the people of Makkah, or all of humanity (according to different interpretations of the above verse) that He has sent them a Messenger from among themselves who they know personally, whose position they are sure of, and who they recognize as truthful and trustworthy. They could not accuse this person of lying or ignore his advice, because he was one of them. Every Arab tribe had some kinship or relation to the Messenger of Allah ﷺ, whether close or distant. Ibn 'Abbās and others understood this as the meaning of the words of Allah Exalted:

---

4 *al-Tawbah*, 128.

5 Naṣr ibn Muhammad al-Samarqandī al-Ḥanafī was a great imam, ascetic, and jurist. He authored *Tanbīh al-Ghāfilīn*, among other works, and he passed away in 375 AH. His biography can be found in *Siyar A'lām al-Nubalā'* (16/322) and elsewhere.

6 This is a non-canonical *shādh* or "anomalous" recitation, transmitted from Fāṭimah and 'Ā'ishah. "*Min anfasikum*" gives the meaning: "From the most excellent among you".

7 Meaning: "From among yourselves".

الباب الأَوَّلُ

فِي ثَنَاءِ اللهِ تَعَالَىٰ عَلَيْهِ وَ إِظْهَارِهِ عَظِيمَ قَدْرِهِ لَدَيْهِ

اعلم أن في كتاب الله العزيز آياتٍ كثيرةً مفصحةً بجميل ذِكْر المصطفى، وعَدِّ محَاسِنه، وتعظيم أَمره، وتنويه قَدْره، اعتمدنا منها على ما ظهر معناه، وبانَ فَحْواه، وجمعنا ذلك في عشرة فصول.

الفَصْلُ الأَوَّلُ

فيما جاء من ذلك مجيءَ المَدح والثناء وتَعداد المحاسن؛ كقوله تعالى: ﴿ لَقَدْ جَاءَكُمْ رَسُولٌ مِّنْ أَنفُسِكُمْ عَزِيزٌ عَلَيْهِ مَا عَنِتُّمْ حَرِيصٌ عَلَيْكُم بِالْمُؤْمِنِينَ رَءُوفٌ رَّحِيمٌ ﴾ [التوبة: ١٢٨].

قال السَّمَرْقَنديُّ(٨) :وقرأ بعضهم: ﴿من أَنْفَسِكم﴾(٩) - بفتح الفاء. وقراءةُ الجمهور بالضم.

قال القاضي الإمام أبو الفضل - رحمه الله(١٠) -: أعلَمَ اللهُ تعالى المؤمنين، أو العرب، أو أهل مكة، أو جميع الناس، على اختلاف المفسرين:

---

(٨) هو الإمام الفقيه الزاهد: نصر بن محمد السمرقندي الحنفي صاحب كتاب «تنبيه الغافلين». وغيره توفى سنة (٣٧٥ هـ). له ترجمة في سير أعلام النبلاء ٣٢٢/١٦ وغيره.

(٩) وهي قراءة شاذة مروية عن فاطمة وعائشة/ قاله القاري ٨١/١.

(١٠) على هامش الأصل : «وفقه الله» نسخة. وأبو الفضل: هو القاضي عياض مصنف هذا الكتاب وهذه العبارة من قول الناسخ، وسيعيدها مراراً.

"only honour for [our] kinship"[8].[9] If we take the reading as '*min anfasikum*', then the verse indicates the position of the Prophet ﷺ as the best of his people, the most honoured, and the most elevated in status. Allah lavishes the most exuberant praise on His Prophet ﷺ. Furthermore, He praises his eagerness to guide his people to Islam, his concern for their affairs in this life and the next, and his mercy and compassion for the believers. Some commentators add that Allah Exalted describes the Prophet ﷺ with two of His Names: "Gracious and Merciful"[10].

Allah Exalted said: "Indeed, Allah has done the believers a [great] favour by raising a Messenger from among them – reciting to them His Revelations, purifying them, and teaching them the Book and wisdom. For indeed they had previously been clearly astray."[11]

In another verse, Allah Exalted says: "He is the One Who raised for the illiterate [people] a Messenger from among themselves – reciting to them His Revelations, purifying them, and teaching them the Book and wisdom, for indeed they had previously been clearly astray."[12]

And: "Since We have sent you a Messenger from among yourselves – reciting to you Our Revelations, purifying you, teaching you the Book and wisdom, and teaching you what you never knew."[13]

'Alī ibn Abī Tālib ﷺ explained the words of Allah Exalted "from among yourselves"[14] to mean: "By lineage, familial kinship through marriage, and background. There was not a single fornicator among

8 *al-Shūrā*, 23.

9 Reported by Bukhārī (4818) and Tirmidhī (3251).

10 *al-Tawbah*, 128.

11 Āl 'Imrān, 164.

12 *al-Jumu'ah*, 2.

13 *al-Baqarah*, 151.

14 ibid.

مَن المواجَهُ بهذا الخطاب أنه بَعَث فيهم رسولًا من أنفُسِهم يعرفونه، ويتحقَّقون مكانه، ويَعلمون صدقَه وأمانته؛ فلا يتهمونه بالكذب، وترْك النصيحة لهم، لكونه منهم، وأنه لم يكن في العرب قبيلة إلَّا ولها على رسول الله ﷺ ولادة أو قَرابة[١١].

٣- وهو عند ابن عباس وغيره معنى قوله تعالى: ﴿إِلَّا الْمَوَدَّةَ فِي الْقُرْبَىٰ﴾[١٢] [الشورى: ٢٣] وكَوْنِهِ من أَشرَفِهم، وَأَرْفَعِهم، وأَفْضلهم، على قراءة الفتح؛ وهذه نهاية المدح؛ ثم وصفه بعدُ بأَوصاف حَميدة، وأثنى عليه بمَحامد كثيرة؛ من حِرْصه على هدايتهم، ورُشدهم، وإسلامهم، وشدة ما يُعنِتُهم[١٣]، يضُرُّ بهم في دُنياهم وأُخراهم، وعزَّتِه عليه[١٤] ورأفته ورحمته بمؤمنيهم. قال بعضُهُم: أَعطاهُ اسْمَيْنِ من أسمائه: رؤوفٌ، رَحيمٌ. ومثلُه (٤/أ) في الآية الأخرىٰ قوله [تعالى]: ﴿لَقَدْ مَنَّ اللَّهُ عَلَى الْمُؤْمِنِينَ إِذْ بَعَثَ فِيهِمْ رَسُولًا مِّنْ أَنفُسِهِمْ يَتْلُو عَلَيْهِمْ آيَاتِهِ وَيُزَكِّيهِمْ وَيُعَلِّمُهُمُ الْكِتَابَ وَالْحِكْمَةَ وَإِن كَانُوا مِن قَبْلُ لَفِي ضَلَالٍ مُّبِينٍ﴾ [آل عمران ١٦٤]. وفي الآية الأخرىٰ: ﴿هُوَ الَّذِي بَعَثَ فِي الْأُمِّيِّينَ رَسُولًا مِّنْهُمْ يَتْلُو عَلَيْهِمْ آيَاتِهِ وَيُزَكِّيهِمْ وَيُعَلِّمُهُمُ الْكِتَابَ وَالْحِكْمَةَ وَإِن كَانُوا مِن قَبْلُ لَفِي ضَلَالٍ مُّبِينٍ﴾ [الجمعة: ٢].

---

(١١) (ولادة أو قرابة): قال القاري: (ولادة): أي قرابة قريبة. (أو قرابة): أي بعيدة.

(١٢) أخرجه البخاري (٤٨١٨)، والترمذي (٣٢٥١).

(١٣) (وشدة ما يعنتهم): أي ما يشق عليهم ولا يطيقونه.

(١٤) كلمة: «عليه» لم ترد في المطبوع.

his ancestors since Adam ﷺ; they were all properly married."[15] Ibn al-Kalbī[16] said: "I wrote down five hundred female ancestors of the Prophet ﷺ and I did not find a single fornicator. Neither did they practice [the immoral customs] of Jāhiliyyah[17]."

Ibn 'Abbās explained the words of Allah Exalted "as well as your movements [in prayer] along with [fellow] worshippers"[18] as: "from Prophet to Prophet, until I sent you as a Prophet."[19]

Ja'far ibn Muhammad[20] said: "Allah knew that His creation would be deficient in their obedience to Him. He informed them of that so they would know they could never achieve absolute purity in serving Him, and he created a being between Himself and His creation from among them, resembling them in form and appearance. He clothed him with His Attributes of mercy and compassion, and sent him to the creation as a sincere and truthful ambassador. He made obedience to him like obedience to Him, and approval from him like approval from Him. Allah Exalted said: 'Whoever obeys the Messenger has truly obeyed Allah.'[21] And: 'We have sent you [O Prophet] only as a mercy for the whole world.'[22]"

---

15 Reported by Ibn Abī 'Umar al-'Adanī in his *Musnad*, and from the same chain by al-Rāmahurmuzī in Al-*Muḥaddith al-Fāṣil bayn al-Rāwī wa al-Wā'ī*. Also reported by Ṭabarānī in *Al-Awsaṭ*. Haythamī said in *Majma' al-Zawā'id* (8/214): "The chain of transmission contains Muhammad ibn Ja'far ibn 'Alī, who Ḥākim declared as *ṣaḥīḥ* in *Al-Mustadrak* after some discussion about him. The rest of the narrators in the chain are trustworthy."

16 Muhammad ibn al-Sā'ib al-Kalbī, an expert in genealogy and *tafsīr*. Ibn Ḥajar said: "He was accused of lying and stubbornness." He passed away in about 146 AH. See *Siyar A'lām al-Nubalā'* (6/248-249).

17 The pre-Islamic "Age of Ignorance".

18 *al-Shu'arā*, 219.

19 Haythamī said in *Majma' al-Zawā'id* (8/214): "It was related by Bazzār, and its narrators are trustworthy." The chain was also authenticated by Suyūṭī in *Al-Manāhil*, p. 7.

20 Commonly known as Ja'far al-Ṣādiq. A veracious scholar and jurist, he died in 148 AH. See *Siyar A'lām al-Nubalā'* (6/255-270).

21 *al-Nisā'*, 80.

22 *al-Anbiyā'*, 107.

وقوله [تعالى]: ﴿كَمَا أَرْسَلْنَا فِيكُمْ رَسُولًا مِّنكُمْ يَتْلُو عَلَيْكُمْ آيَاتِنَا وَيُزَكِّيكُمْ وَيُعَلِّمُكُمُ الْكِتَابَ وَالْحِكْمَةَ وَيُعَلِّمُكُم مَّا لَمْ تَكُونُوا تَعْلَمُونَ﴾ [البقرة: ١٥١].

٤- ورُوي عن عليّ بن أبي طالب، عنه - صلوات الله عليه - في قوله تعالى: ﴿مِنْ أَنْفَسِكم﴾ قال: «نَسباً وصِهراً وحسَباً؛ ليس في آبائي من لَدُن آدم سِفَاح، كُلُّنا نِكاح»[١٥]. [قال ابنُ الكلبي: كَتبتُ للنبي ﷺ خَمْس مئة أُمّ، فما وجَدتُ فيهن سِفَاحاً ولا شيئاً مما كان عليه الجاهلية.

٥- وعن ابن عباس في قوله تعالى: ﴿وَتَقَلُّبَكَ فِي السَّاجِدِينَ﴾ [الشعراء: ٢١٩] قال: مِنْ نَبيّ إلىٰ نَبيّ، حتى أَخرجَك نبيّاً]. وقال جَعْفر بن محمد[١٦]: عَلِم اللهُ عجْزَ خَلْقِه عن طاعتِه، فعرَّفَهم ذلك؛ لكي يَعلَمُوا أَنَّهم لا ينالون الصفو من خدمته؛ فأقام بينهم وبينه مخلوقاً من جنسهم في الصُّورة، وألبسه من نَعْتِه الرأفةَ والرحمة، وأخرجَهُ إلىٰ الخَلْقِ سفيراً صادقاً، وجعل طاعته طاعتَهُ، وموافقته موافقتَه؛ فقال [تعالى]: ﴿مَّن يُطِعِ الرَّسُولَ فَقَدْ أَطَاعَ اللَّهَ﴾ [النساء: ٨٠] وقال الله تعالى ﴿وَمَا أَرْسَلْنَاكَ إِلَّا رَحْمَةً لِّلْعَالَمِينَ﴾ [الأنبياء: ١٠٧]. قال أبو بكر بن طاهر:

(١٥) أخرجه ابن أبي عمر العدني في مسنده، ومن طريقه الرامَهُرْمُزي في «الفاصل بين الراوي والواعي». وأخرجه أيضاً الطبراني في الأوسط. قال الهيثمي في مجمع الزوائد ٢١٤/٨: «فيه محمد بن جعفر بن علي، صحَّح له الحاكم في المستدرك، وقد تكلم فيه، وبقية رجاله ثقات».

(١٦) جعفر بن محمد: هو المعروف بالصادق، صدوق، فقيه، إمام. مات سنة (١٤٨). انظر ترجمته في سير أعلام النبلاء ٢٥٥/٦-٢٧٠.

Abū Bakr ibn Ṭāhir said: "Allah Exalted beautified Muhammad ﷺ with the quality of mercy, until his very existence and all of his characteristics were a mercy to the creation. Whoever is touched by a part of his mercy is saved in the two abodes[23] from every misfortune and connected to every desired thing. Do you not see that Allah Exalted says: 'We have sent you [O Prophet] only as a mercy for the whole world'[24]? His life was a mercy, and so was his death." Just as the Prophet ﷺ said: "My life is goodness for you, and so is my death."[25]

The Prophet ﷺ also said: "When Allah wishes mercy for a nation, He takes their Prophet [back to Him] before them, and makes him an example for them to follow and a harbinger of their success."[26] Al-Samarqandī said that the Mercy of Allah is "a mercy for the whole world"[27] i.e., for both human beings and jinn. It is also said to refer to all of creation. The Prophet ﷺ is a mercy to the believer by guiding them, to the hypocrite by saving them from being killed, and to the disbeliever by delaying their punishment.

Ibn 'Abbās ﷺ said: "He is a mercy to both believers and disbelievers, [the latter of whom] are saved from [the immediate punishment] sent down to other [disbelieving] nations for their lies."

It was reported that the Prophet ﷺ said to Jibrīl ﷺ: "Has this mercy affected you in any way?" He replied: "Yes. I used to fear my outcome, but now I feel safe because of the way Allah ﷻ praised me when He said: 'full of power, held in honour by the Lord of the

---

23 i.e., this life and the Hereafter.

24 *al-Anbiyā'*, 107.

25 Reported by Bazzār in *Kashf al-Astār* (845) from Ibn Mas'ūd. Haythamī said in *Majma' al-Zawā'id* (9/24): "Its narrators are reliable." Authenticated by Suyūṭī in *Al-Manāhil*, p. 8. See also *Fayḍ al-Qadīr* (3/401).

26 Reported by Muslim (2288) from the hadith of Abū Mūsā al-Ash'arī.

27 *al-Anbiyā'*, 107.

زَيَّنَ اللّٰهُ [تعالى] محمداً ﷺ بزينة الرحمة؛ فكان كونُهُ[١٧] رحمة، وجميع شمائله وصفاتِه رحمةً على الخَلْقِ؛ فمن أَصَابه شيء من رحمته فهو الناجي في الدَّارَيْنِ من كلِّ مكروه، والواصلُ فيهما إلى كل محبوب؛ ألا ترى أنَّ اللّٰه تعالى يقولُ: ﴿وَمَا أَرْسَلْنَاكَ إِلَّا رَحْمَةً لِّلْعَالَمِينَ﴾ [الأنبياء: ١٠٧]؛ فكانت حياتُه رحمةً، ومماتهُ رحمةً.

٦- كما قال عليه السلام: «حَيَاتي خيرٌ لكم ومَوْتي خيرٌ لكم»[١٨].

٧- وكما قال [عليه الصلاة والسلام]: «إذا أراد اللّٰهُ رحمةً بأُمَّةٍ قَبض نبيَّها قَبْلها فجعله لها فَرَطاً وسَلَفاً»[١٩]. وقال السَّمَرْقَنْدِي رحمه الله: ﴿رحمةً للعالمين﴾: يعني للإنس والجنّ. وقيل لجميع الخَلق؛ للمؤمن رحمة بالهداية، ورحمةً للمنافق بالأمانِ في القَتْلِ، ورحمةً للكافر بتأخير العذاب. قال ابنُ عباس [رضي الله عنهما]: هو رحمةٌ للمؤمنينَ وللكافرين؛ إذ عُوفُوا مما أَصابَ غَيْرهم من الأمم المكذّبة.

٨- وحُكي أنَّ النبيَّ ﷺ قال لجبريل عليه السلام: «هل أصابكَ من هذه الرحمة شيءٌ؟» قال «نعم؛ كنتُ أَخْشى العاقبة فأمِنْتُ لِثَناءِ اللّٰه عزَّ وجلَّ عليَّ بقوله: ﴿ذِى قُوَّةٍ عِندَ ذِى الْعَرْشِ مَكِينٍ (٢٠) مُّطَاعٍ ثَمَّ

---

(١٧) كَوْنُهُ: وُجُوْدُهُ.

(١٨) أخرجه البزار (٨٤٥) كشف الأستار من حديث ابن مسعود. قال الهيثمي في مجمع الزوائد ٢٤/٩: «رجاله رجال الصحيح» وصححه السيوطي في مناهل الصفا (٨)، وانظر فيض القدير (٤٠١/٣).

(١٩) أخرجه مسلم (٢٢٨٨) من حديث أبي موسىٰ الأشعري. (فرطاً) بمعنى الفارط: المتقدم إلى الماء لِيُهَيِّءَ السقي. يريد أنه شفيع يتقدم. (سلفاً): هو المُقدَّمُ

Throne, obeyed there [in heaven], and trustworthy.'[28]"[29]

Ja'far ibn Muhammad al-Ṣādiq interpreted the words of Allah Exalted: "Greetings [*salām*] to you from the people of the right"[30] as referring to safety and tranquillity rather than greetings. He said: "The cause of their tranquillity is the distinction and honour of Muhammad ﷺ."

Allah Exalted said: "Allah is the Light of the heavens and the earth. His Light is like a niche in which there is a lamp, the lamp is in a crystal, the crystal is like a shining star, lit from [the oil of] a blessed olive tree, [located] neither to the east nor the west, whose oil would almost glow, even without being touched by fire. Light upon Light! Allah guides whoever He wills to His Light. And Allah sets forth parables for humanity. For Allah has [perfect] knowledge of all things."[31]

Ka'b[32] and Ibn Jubayr[33] interpreted the second reference to "light" in the verse[34] as the light of Muhammad ﷺ. Sahl ibn 'Abdullāh[35] said: "The meaning of the verse is: 'Allah guides the people of the heavens and the earth. The light from the loins of Muhammad ﷺ is

---

28 *al-Takwīr*, 20-21.

29 Suyūṭī said in *Al-Manāhil*, p. 11: "I did not find this narration."

30 *al-Wāqi'ah*, 91.

31 *al-Nūr*, 35.

32 Ka'b al-Aḥbār was a knowledgeable Jewish rabbi who converted to Islam after the death of the Prophet ﷺ. Ka'b passed away towards the end of the Caliphate of 'Uthmān. See *Siyar A'lām al-Nubalā'* (3/489).

33 Sa'īd ibn Jubayr was firm, trustworthy, and a scholar of jurisprudence from the Followers. He was killed by Al-Ḥajjāj ibn Yūsuf in 95 AH. See *Siyar A'lām al-Nubalā'* (4/321-343).

34 i.e., "His Light is like..." (*al-Nūr*, 35).

35 Sahl ibn 'Abdullāh al-Tustarī, a *ṣūfī* and ascetic. He passed away in 283 AH. See *Siyar A'lām al-Nubalā'* (13/330).

أَمِينٍ﴾[٢٠] [التكوير: ٢٠، ٢١]. ورُوي عن جَعْفر بن محمد (٥/أ) الصادق في قوله تعالى: ﴿فَسَلَامٌ لَّكَ مِنْ أَصْحَابِ الْيَمِينِ﴾ [الواقعة: ٩١] أي بكَ؛ إنما وَقعَتْ سلامتهم مِنْ أجل كرامة محمد ﷺ. وقال الله تعالى ﴿اللَّهُ نُورُ السَّمَاوَاتِ وَالْأَرْضِ ۚ مَثَلُ نُورِهِ كَمِشْكَاةٍ فِيهَا مِصْبَاحٌ ۖ الْمِصْبَاحُ فِي زُجَاجَةٍ ۖ الزُّجَاجَةُ كَأَنَّهَا كَوْكَبٌ دُرِّيٌّ يُوقَدُ مِن شَجَرَةٍ مُّبَارَكَةٍ زَيْتُونَةٍ لَّا شَرْقِيَّةٍ وَلَا غَرْبِيَّةٍ يَكَادُ زَيْتُهَا يُضِيءُ وَلَوْ لَمْ تَمْسَسْهُ نَارٌ ۚ نُّورٌ عَلَىٰ نُورٍ ۗ يَهْدِي اللَّهُ لِنُورِهِ مَن يَشَاءُ ۚ وَيَضْرِبُ اللَّهُ الْأَمْثَالَ لِلنَّاسِ ۗ وَاللَّهُ بِكُلِّ شَيْءٍ عَلِيمٌ﴾ [النور: ٣٥]. قال كعبٌ[٢١]، وابن جُبير[٢٢]: المراد بالنور الثاني - هنا - محمدٌ عليه السلام. وقوله تعالى ﴿مَثَلُ نُورِهِ﴾ أي: نور محمدٍ ﷺ. وقال سَهْلُ بنُ عبدِ اللهِ[٢٣]: المعنى اللهُ هادي أهل السموات والأرض؛ ثم قال مَثَلُ نورِ محمد إذ كان مستودعاً في الأصلاب كَمِشكَاة صفتها كذا؛ وأراد بالمصباح: قلبَه وبالزجاجة[٢٤] صدره؛ أي: كأنه كوكبٌ دُرِّيٌّ لما فيه من الإيمان

---

(٢٠) قال السيوطي في المناهل (١١): لم أجده.

(٢١) هو كعب الأحبار، علامة حِبْر، كان يهودياً فأسلم بعد وفاة النبي ﷺ. مات في أواخر خلافة عثمان. انظر ترجمته في سير أعلام النبلاء ٤٨٩/٣.

(٢٢) ابن جبير هو سعيد. تابعي ثقة ثبت فقيه. قتل بين يدي الحجاج سنة (٩٥ هـ). انظر ترجمته في سير أعلام النبلاء ٣٢١/٤-٣٤٣

(٢٣) هو سهل بن عبد الله التُسْتري، الصوفي الزاهد. مات سنة (٢٨٣ هـ). انظر ترجمته في سير أعلام النبلاء ٣٣٠/١٣.

(٢٤) في الأصل «والزجاجة» والمثبت من المطبوع.

"like a niche"[36]. The "lamp"[37] is his heart. The "crystal"[38] is his chest, which is "like a shining star"[39] because of the faith and wisdom it contains. His chest is "lit from [the oil of] a blessed tree"[40], meaning from the light of Ibrāhīm ﷺ, "whose oil would almost glow"[41], i.e., the glow of his prophethood was evident even before he spoke."

Other interpretations of this verse have also been recorded, and Allah knows best.

On other occasions, Allah Exalted refers to the Prophet ﷺ as "a light", or "a beacon of light". He says: "There certainly has come to you from Allah a light and a clear Book."[42] And: "O Prophet! We have sent you as a witness, and a deliverer of good news, and a warner, and a caller to [the Way of] Allah by His Command, and a beacon of light."[43]

Allah Exalted says, in Surah al-Sharḥ: "Have We not uplifted your heart for you [O Prophet], relieved you of the burden which weighed so heavily on your back, and elevated your renown for you? So, surely with hardship comes ease. Surely with [that] hardship comes [more] ease. So once you have fulfilled [your duty], strive [in devotion], turning to your Lord [alone] with hope."[44]

In the first verse of the surah, the verb "*sharaḥa*" (translated above as "uplifted") means "to expand". "*Ṣadr*", which usually means "chest", refers here to the heart of the Prophet ﷺ. Ibn ʿAbbās said:

---

36 *al-Nūr*, 35.

37 ibid.

38 ibid.

39 ibid.

40 ibid.

41 ibid.

42 *al-Mā'idah*, 15.

43 *al-Aḥzāb*, 45-46.

44 *al-Sharḥ*, 1-8.

والحكمة ﴿يُوقَدُ مِن شَجَرَةٍ مُّبَارَكَةٍ﴾ أي: من نور إبراهيم. وضرب المَثَل بالشجرة المباركة.

وقوله ﴿يَكَادُ زَيْتُهَا يُضِيءُ﴾ أي: تكاد نبوّة محمد ﷺ تبينُ للناس قَبْل كلامه كهذا الزيت. وقد[٢٥] قيل في هذه الآية غير هذا. والله أعلم.

وقد سماه الله تعالى في القرآن في غير هذا الموضع نوراً، وسراجاً منيراً؛ فقال [تعالى]: ﴿قَدْ جَاءَكُم مِّنَ اللَّهِ نُورٌ وَكِتَابٌ مُّبِينٌ﴾ [المائدة: ١٥].

وقال [تعالى]: ﴿إِنَّا أَرْسَلْنَاكَ شَاهِدًا وَمُبَشِّرًا وَنَذِيرًا (٤٥) وَدَاعِيًا إِلَى اللَّهِ بِإِذْنِهِ وَسِرَاجًا مُّنِيرًا﴾ [الأحزاب: ٤٥، ٤٦].

ومن هذا قولهُ تعالى: ﴿أَلَمْ نَشْرَحْ لَكَ صَدْرَكَ (١) وَوَضَعْنَا عَنكَ وِزْرَكَ (٢) الَّذِي أَنقَضَ ظَهْرَكَ (٣) وَرَفَعْنَا لَكَ ذِكْرَكَ (٤) فَإِنَّ مَعَ الْعُسْرِ يُسْرًا (٥) إِنَّ مَعَ الْعُسْرِ يُسْرًا (٦) فَإِذَا فَرَغْتَ فَانصَبْ (٧) وَإِلَىٰ رَبِّكَ فَارْغَب (٨)﴾ [الشرح].

شَرَحَ: وَسَّع: والمراد بالصَّدْر هنا: القَلْب. قال ابنُ عباس: شرحه بالإسلام.

وقال سَهلٌ: بنورِ الرسالة.

وقال الحسن[٢٦] : مَلأَه حُكماً وعِلماً.

---

(٢٥) «قد»، لم ترد في المطبوع.

(٢٦) الحسن: هو البصري، تابعي. ثقة فقيه فاضل مشهور. مات سنة (١١٠ هـ). ترجمه العلامة أبو الحسن

"He opened his chest with Islam." Sahl said: "...with the light of Messengership." And al-Ḥasan al-Baṣrī[45] commented: "He filled it with wisdom and knowledge." The verse was also interpreted as: "Have We not purified your heart so that you are not harmed by *waswās*[46]."

The second and third verses, "relieved you of the burden which weighed so heavily on your back"[47], were said to refer to his mistakes before prophethood. The "burden"[48] was also interpreted as the baggage of Jāhiliyyah. Al-Māwardī[49] and al-Sulamī[50] said it referred to the Divine Message which would weigh down on him until he was able to convey it to others. Al-Samarqandī understood the verse to mean: "We have protected you, and had we not, the burden of your mistakes would have weighed heavily on your back."

Commenting on the fourth verse, "and elevated your renown for you?"[51], Yaḥyā ibn Adam[52] said: "[meaning,] with Prophethood." It was also said to refer to the statement "*lā ilāha il Allāh, Muhammad rasūl Allāh*"[53]; or the *adhān*[54], which also includes the mention of Allah Exalted followed by the mention of the Prophet ﷺ.

The decision of Allah ﷻ to connect His Name with that of His

---

45 The famous jurist and upstanding narrator from the followers. He died in 110 AH. Abū al-Ḥasan al-Nadwī wrote a biography of him in *Rijāl al-Fikr wa al-Da'wah fī al-Islām*. There is also a detailed biography in *Siyar A'lām al-Nubalā'* (4/563).

46 "*Waswās*": the whispers of Shayṭān.

47 *al-Sharḥ*, 2-3.

48 *al-Sharḥ*, 2.

49 'Alī ibn Muhammad al-Māwardī, author of *Al-Ḥāwī*, *Al-Aḥkām al-Sulṭāniyyah*, and other texts. He died in 450 AH. See *Siyar A'lām al-Nubalā'* (18/64).

50 Muhammad ibn al-Ḥusayn al-Sulamī. A devout scholar and expert in hadith. Dhahabī said: "His works include fabricated hadiths and stories." He died in 412 AH. See *Siyar A'lām al-Nubalā'* (17/247).

51 *al-Sharḥ*, 4.

52 A noble scholar and *ḥāfiẓ*. He died in approximately in 203 AH.

53 "There is no-one worthy of worship except Allah, [and] Muhammad is the Messenger of Allah."

54 The call to prayer.

وقيل: معناه ألم نُطَهر قلبك حتى لا يؤذيك الوسواس؟

﴿وَوَضَعْنَا عَنكَ وِزْرَكَ (٢) الَّذِى أَنقَضَ ظَهْرَكَ (٣)﴾ قيل: ما سلف من ذَنْبِك، يعني: قبل النبوَّة.

وقيل: أراد ثِقَلَ أيام الجاهلية.

وقيل: أراد ما أثقل ظَهْرَه من الرسالة حتى بلَّغها. حكاه الماوَرْدِيُّ[٢٧] والسُّلَمِيُّ[٢٨].

وقيل: عَصَمْنَاك، ولولا ذلك لأثقلتِ الذنوبُ ظهرك؛ حكاه السَّمَرْقَنْدي.

﴿وَرَفَعْنَا لَكَ ذِكْرَكَ﴾ قال يحيىٰ بن آدم[٢٩]: بالنبوة (٥/ب) وقيل: إذا ذُكِرْتُ ذُكِرْتَ معي، قَوْلَ لا إله إلا الله، محمد رسول الله. وقيل: في الأذان.

قال الفقيه القاضي أبو الفَضْل رحمه الله: هذا تقريرٌ مِنَ الله جلَّ اسْمُه لنبيِّه ﷺ على عَظِيم نعمه لَدَيْه، وشَرِيف مَنْزِلَته عِنْدَه، وكرامتهِ عليه؛ بأَنْ شرحَ قَلْبه للإيمان والهداية، وَوَسَّعَهُ لِوَعْي العِلْمِ، وَحملِ الحِكْمَة، ورَفَعَ عنه ثِقَلَ أُمورِ الجاهلية عليه، وبغَّضَهُ لِسِيَرِها، وما كانَتْ عليه

النَّدْوي في كتابه «رجال الفكر والدعوة في الإسلام». وله ترجمة مطولة في سير أعلام النبلاء ٥٦٣/٤.

(٢٧) الماوردي: هو علي بن محمد. صاحب كتاب «الحاوي» و « الأحكام السلطانية» وغيره. مات سنة (٤٥٠ هـ). انظر ترجمته في سير أعلام النبلاء ٦٤/١٨.

(٢٨) السُّلَمِيُّ: هو محمد بن الحسين، إمام حافظ محدث، صوفي. قال الذهبي: «في تصانيفه أحاديث وحكايات موضوعة». مات سنة (٤١٢ هـ). انظر ترجمته في سير أعلام النبلاء ٢٤٧/١٧.

(٢٩) يحيى بن آدم، ثقة حافظ فاضل مات سنة (٢٠٣ هـ) (التقريب).

Prophet ﷺ confirms the magnitude of the blessings He bestowed upon him, and his noble station with Him. It also reflects the high esteem of Allah Exalted for His Prophet ﷺ. He opened his heart to faith and guidance, expanded his chest with the ultimate knowledge, and endowed him with wisdom and understanding. He removed the baggage of pre-Islamic ignorance and made chasing the affairs of Jāhiliyyah disliked to the Prophet ﷺ, and caused His Religion to prevail over all others. He lightened the heavy load of Prophethood and Messengership, enabling him to communicate to the people that which had been sent down to them. Allah Exalted emphasized the lofty rank and status of His Prophet ﷺ, elevated his renown, and joined his name with His own.

Qatādah[55] said: "Allah has elevated the mention [of the Prophet ﷺ] in this life and the Hereafter. Anyone who wishes to give an address[56], witness a contract, or perform the prayer, must utter the words "*ashhadu an lā ilāha il Allāh, wa ashhadu anna Muhammad rasūl Allāh*"[57].

Abū Sa'īd al-Khudrī related that the Prophet ﷺ said: "Jibrīl ﷺ came to me and said: 'My Lord and your Lord said to me: 'Do you know how I raised the mention [of the Prophet ﷺ]?' I replied: 'Allah and His Messenger know best.' He said: 'When I am mentioned, [the Prophet ﷺ] is mentioned with Me.'''[58]

Ibn 'Aṭā'[59] said: "[Allah Exalted] said: 'I have made your mention

---

55 Qatādah ibn Di'āmah al-Sadūsī, a reliable and trustworthy man from the Followers. He died in the 110s AH. See *Siyar A'lām al-Nubalā'* (5/269).

56 A "*khutbah*", or "Friday sermon".

57 The *shahādah*, or profession of faith: "I bear witness that there is no-one worthy of worship except Allah, and I bear witness that Muhammad is the Messenger of Allah."

58 Reported by Abū Ya'lā (1380) and others. Authenticated by Ibn Ḥibbān in *Mawārid al-Ẓam'ān* (1772), Ḍiyā' in *Al-Mukhtārah*, and Suyūṭī in *Al-Jāmi' al-Ṣaghīr* (83). Haythamī graded the chain as *ḥasan* in *Majma' al-Zawā'id* (8/254).

59 Aḥmad ibn Muhamad ibn Sahl ibn 'Aṭā', a devout and pious worshipper. He passed away in 309 AH. See *Siyar A'lām al-Nubalā'* (14/255).

بظهور دِيْنِهِ على الدِّين كُلِّه، وحَطَّ عنه عُهدةَ أَعباءِ الرسالة والنبوَّة لتبليغه للناس ما نُزِّل إليهم، وتَنويهه بعظيم مَكانه، وجَلِيل رُتْبَته، ورفعه ذِكْرَه، وقِرَانه[٣٠] مع اسمِهِ اسْمَه. قال قَتَادةُ[٣١]: رفَع اللهُ ذِكْرَهُ في الدُّنيا والآخِرة فليس خطيبٌ ولا متشهِّدٌ ولا صاحبُ صلاةٍ إلَّا يقول: أَشهدُ أَنْ لا إله إلا الله وأن محمَّداً رسولُ الله.

٩- وروَىٰ أبو سَعيد الخُدْرِي أن النبي ﷺ قال: «أَتاني جبريلُ عليه السلام، فقال: إن ربِّي وربَّك يقولُ: تَدْرِي كيف رفعتُ ذِكْرك؟ قلتُ: اللهُ ورسوله أَعْلَم. قال إذا ذُكِرتُ ذُكِرتَ معي»[٣٢].

قال ابنُ عطاء[٣٣]: جعلتُ تَمام الإيمان بذِكْري معك.

وقال أيضاً: جعلتُكَ ذكراً من ذِكْري، فمَنْ ذَكَرك ذَكَرني.

وقال جَعْفَرُ بنُ محمد الصادق: لا يذكرك أحد بالرسالة إلَّا ذكرني بالربوبيّة.

وأشار بعضهم في ذلك إلى الشفاعة.

وَمِنْ ذِكْرِه معه تعالى أن قَرَن طاعتهَ بطاعته واسْمَه باسْمِهِ؛ فقال تعالى: ﴿وَأَطِيعُواْ اللهَ وَالرَّسُولَ﴾ [آل عمران: ١٣٢]. و﴿ءَامِنُواْ بِاللهِ وَرَسُولِهِ﴾

---

(٣٠) وقِرانه: وجَمْعِهِ.

(٣١) هو قتادة بن دعامة السدوسي، تابعي ثقة ثبت. مات سنة بضع عشرةَ ومئة. مترجم في السير ٢٦٩/٥.

(٣٢) أخرجه أبو يعلى (١٣٨٠) وغيره، وصححه ابن حبان (١٧٧٢) موارد الظمآن، والضياء في «المختارة»، والسيوطي في الجامع الصغير (٨٣)، وحسَّن إسناده الهيثمي في مجمع الزوائد ٢٥٤/٨.

(٣٣) هو الزاهد العابد أحمد بن محمد بن سهل بن عطاء. مات سنة (٣٠٩ هـ). انظر ترجمته في سير أعلام النبلاء (٢٥٥/١٤).

being connected to Mine a completion of īmān.'" He also reported: "[Allah Exalted] said: 'I have made your remembrance a part of My remembrance, so whoever remembers you has remembered Me.'" Ja'far ibn Muhammad al-Ṣādiq reported: "[Allah Exalted] said: 'Anyone that mentions you as the Messenger mentions Me as the Lord.'"

Allah Exalted connects the name of the Prophet ﷺ to His Name, and obedience to the Prophet ﷺ with obedience to Him. He says in the Qur'an: "Obey Allah and the Messenger".[60] And: "Believe in Allah and His Messenger".[61] In both verses, the words "Allah" and "the/His Messenger" are connected with the *wāw al-'aṭf*, the conjunction of partnership. Indeed, it would be impermissible to use this type of grammatical construction in connection with Allah Exalted for anyone except for the Prophet ﷺ.

I was permitted to relate the following hadith by Abū 'Alī al-Ḥusayn ibn Muhammad al-Jayyānī, who said: "It was narrated from Abū 'Umar al-Namarī, from Abū Muhammad ibn 'Abd al-Mu'min, from Abū Bakr ibn Dāsah, from Abū Dāwūd al-Sijzī[62], from Abū al-Walīd al-Ṭayālisī, from Shu'bah, from Manṣūr, from 'Abdullāh ibn Yasār, from Ḥudhayfah, from the Prophet ﷺ, who said: 'None of you should say "Whatever Allah wishes and[63] so-and-so wishes." Rather, you should say: "Whatever Allah wishes, then, so-and-so wishes."'"[64]

Al-Khaṭṭābī[65] said: "The Prophet ﷺ guided them to the correct practice of giving precedence to the will of Allah. He chose the word

---

60 Āl 'Imrān, 132.

61 *al-Ḥadīd*, 7.

62 Abū Dāwūd al-Sijistānī.

63 The word used for "and", "*wa*", functions as the *wāw al-*'aṭf in this sentence.

64 Reported here from the chain of Abū Dāwūd (4980). Also reported by Nasā'ī in 'Amal *al-Yawm wa al-Laylah* (985), Ibn al-Sunnī (666), and Aḥmad (5/384). Authenticated by Nawawī in *Al-Adhkār* (1183) and *Riyāḍ al-Ṣāliḥīn* (1838), with his commentary on both occasions.

65 Ḥamd ibn Muhammad Abū Sulaymān al-Khaṭṭābī, an imam and *ḥāfiẓ*. He died in 388 AH. See *Siyar A'lām al-Nubalā'* (17/23).

[الحديد: ٧]؛ فجمع بينهما بواو العطف المُشَرِّكة.

ولا يجوز جَمعُ هذا الكلام في غير حقّه عليه السلام.

١٠- حدثنا الشيخ أبو علي: الحُسين بنُ محمد الجيّاني الحافظ فيما أجازَنيه، وقرأتهُ على الثّقة عنه. قال: حدثنا أبو عُمَرَ النَّمَرِيُّ؛ قال حدثنا أبو محمد بن عبد المؤمن، حدثنا أبو بكر بن داسةَ، حدثنا أبو داود السِّجْزِيُّ، حدثنا أبو الوليد الطَّيالِسِيُّ، حدثنا (٦/أ) شُعبة، عن منصور، عن عبد اللهِ بن يَسَار، عن حُذَيفَةَ، عن النبي ﷺ؛ قال: «لا يَقُولَنَّ أحدُكم ما شاءَ اللهُ وشاءَ فُلانٌ، ولكن ما شاءَ اللهُ، ثم شَاءَ فلان»[٣٤].

قال الخطَّابي[٣٥]. أرشدهم ﷺ إلى الأدب في تقديم مشيئة الله تعالى على مشيئة مَنْ سِواه، واختارها بـ«ثم» التي هي للنَّسَق والتراخِي، بخلاف الواو التي هي للاشتراك.

١١- ومثله الحديثُ الآخر: إن خطيباً خطب عند النبي ﷺ، فقال: مَنْ يُطِعِ اللهَ ورَسُوله فقد رَشَد، وَمَنْ يَعْصِهما[٣٦]. فقال له النبيُّ ﷺ: «بِئْسَ

---

(٣٤) أسنده المصنف من طريق أبي داود (٤٩٨٠). وأخرجه أيضاً النسائي في «عمل اليوم والليلة» (٩٨٥)، وابن السني (٦٦٦)، وأحمد ٣٨٤/٥ وصححه النووي في الأذكار برقم (١١٨٣)، وفي رياض الصالحين (١٨٣٨) كلاهما بتحقيقي.

(٣٥) هو حَمْد بن محمد: أبو سليمان الخطَّابي، إمام حافظ توفي سنة (٣٨٨ هـ). انظر ترجمته في سير أعلام النبلاء ٢٣/١٧.

(٣٦) على هامش الأصل زيادة: «فقد غوى». ولم أثبتها في المتن لأن لفظ الحديث لأبي داود، ولم ترد فيه.

'*thumma*' (meaning 'then'), which implies sequence and deference, rather than the *wāw* (i.e., '*wa*', meaning 'and'), which implies partnership." Another hadith mentions: "A person was giving an address in the presence of the Prophet ﷺ, and he said: 'Whoever obeys Allah and His Messenger has been guided, and whoever disobeys them both'. The Prophet ﷺ said: 'You are the worst speaker! Go!'"[66] Abū Sulaymān mentions: "He hated the fact that the man had referred to him and Allah Exalted with one word,[67] because of the equivalence it implied." Others stated that he simply objected to the man pausing on the phrase "disobeys them both". The opinion of Abū Sulaymān is more correct, because in another version of the hadith, the man ends with "...and whoever disobeys them both has gone astray", and it does not mention him pausing after "disobeys them both".[68] The scholars of *tafsīr* differed over the meaning of the words of Allah Exalted: "Indeed, Allah showers His blessings upon the Prophet, and His Angels pray for him."[69] Does the verb "*yuṣallūn*" ("they pray") refer to Allah and His Angels? Some commentators allowed this interpretation, but others rejected it on the basis that it would imply partnership by referring to Allah Exalted and part of His creation within one word. They argue that the verse employs the grammatical tool of ellipsis, and "*yuṣallūn*" refers solely to the angels. It was narrated that 'Umar ﷺ said [to the Prophet ﷺ]: "From the honour Allah has bestowed upon you, He has made obedience to you, obedience to Him." As Allah Exalted said: "Whoever obeys the Messenger has truly obeyed Allah."[70]

---

66 Reported by Abū Dāwūd (4981) with this wording, and al-Nasā'ī (6/90), both from the hadith of 'Adiyy ibn Ḥātim.

67 In the Arabic, the phrase "disobeys them both" is conveyed in one word.

68 Reported by Muslim (870).

69 *al-Aḥzāb*, 56.

70 *al-Nisā'*, 80.

خطيبُ القوم أَنتَ! قُمْ» أو قال: «اذهَب»[٣٧]. قال أبو سليمانَ: كَرِهَ منه الجَمْعَ بينَ الاسمين بحَرْفِ الكناية لما فيه من التسويةِ.

وذهب غَيْرُه إلى أنه إنما كَرِه له الوقوفَ على «يَعْصِهما».

١٢- وقولُ أَبي سليمان أَصَحُّ؛ لما رُوِي في الحديث الصحيح أنه قال: «ومَنْ يَعْصِهما فقد غَوَى»[٣٨]. ولم يذكر الوقوف على «يعصِهما».

وقد اختلف المفسِّرون وأصحابُ المعاني في قوله [تعالى]: ﴿إِنَّ اللَّهَ وَمَلَائِكَتَهُ يُصَلُّونَ عَلَى النَّبِيِّ﴾ [الأحزاب: ٥٦]؛ هل ﴿يُصَلُّونَ﴾ راجعة على الله تعالى والملائكةِ أم لا؟.

فأجازَهُ بعضُهم، ومَنَعَهُ آخَرون، لِعِلَّة التشريك، وخَصُّوا الضمير بالملائكة؛ وقَدَّرُوا الآية: إنَّ اللهَ يصلِّي، وملائكته يُصلون.

١٣- وقد روي عن عُمر رَضِيَ اللهُ عَنْهُ أنه قال: مِنْ فَضيلتك عنْد الله أَنْ جعلِ طاعتَك طاعَتَهُ؛ فقال [تعالى]: ﴿مَّن يُطِعِ الرَّسُولَ فَقَدْ أَطَاعَ اللَّهَ﴾[٣٩] [النساء: ٨٠]. وقد قال [تعالى]: ﴿قُلْ إِن كُنتُمْ تُحِبُّونَ اللَّهَ فَاتَّبِعُونِي يُحْبِبْكُمُ اللَّهُ وَيَغْفِرْ لَكُمْ ذُنُوبَكُمْ ۗ وَاللَّهُ غَفُورٌ رَّحِيمٌ (٣١) قُلْ أَطِيعُوا اللَّهَ وَالرَّسُولَ ۖ فَإِن تَوَلَّوْا فَإِنَّ اللَّهَ لَا يُحِبُّ الْكَافِرِينَ﴾ [آل عمران: ٣١، ٣٢].

---

(٣٧) أخرجه أبو داود (٤٩٨١) واللفظ له، والنسائي ٦/٩٠ من حديث عدي بن حاتم وانظر الرواية التالية.

(٣٨) أخرجه مسلم برقم (٨٧٠).

(٣٩) قال السيوطي في المناهل (١٨): «لم أجده».

Allah Exalted also revealed: "Say, [O Prophet,] 'If you [sincerely] love Allah, then follow me; Allah will love you and forgive your sins. For Allah is All-Forgiving, Most Merciful.' Say, [O Prophet,] 'Obey Allah and His Messenger.' If they still turn away, then truly Allah does not like the disbelievers."[71] It is related the when the first verse was sent down, people started to say: "Muhammad wants us to take him as a mercy and a blessing, just as the Christians took 'Īsā." So, Allah Exalted revealed: "Say, [O Prophet,] 'Obey Allah and His Messenger'"[72], again connecting obedience to the Prophet to obedience to Him, despite their accusations. The scholars of *tafsīr* also differed over the meaning of the verses from Surah al-Fātiḥah: "Guide us along the Straight Path, the Path of those You have blessed – not those You are displeased with, or those who are astray."[73] Abū al-Ḥasan al-Māwardī mentioned that Abū al-ʿĀliyah[74] and al-Ḥasan al-Baṣrī both took the opinion that "the Straight Path"[75] refers to the Messenger of Allah ﷺ, his blessed family, and his Companions. Makkī related similar views from the two of them, and commented himself: "It refers to the Messenger of Allah ﷺ and his two Companions, Abū Bakr and 'Umar ﷺ."

Abū al-Layth al-Samarqandī narrated something similar from Abū al-ʿĀliyah regarding the words of Allah Exalted: "The Path of those You have blessed"[76]. He added: "Al-Ḥasan al-Baṣrī heard [what Abū al-ʿĀliyah had said about the verse] and he said: 'I swear by Allah, he has told the truth and advised well.'" Al-Māwardī related the same interpretation of the verse from 'Abd al-Raḥmān ibn Zayd.

---

71 Āl ʿImrān, 31-32.

72 Āl ʿImrān, 32.

73 *al-Fātiḥah*, 6-7.

74 Rufayʿ ibn Mihrān al-Riyāḥī, a respected Follower. He died in 90 or 93 AH.

75 *al-Fātiḥah*, 6.

76 *al-Fātiḥah*, 7.

١٤- ورُوي أنه لما نزلت هذه الآيةُ قالوا: إنَّ محمداً يريد أن نتَّخِذه حنَاناً[٤٠] كما اتخذت النصارى عيسىٰ، فأنزلَ اللهُ [تعالى]: ﴿قُلْ أَطِيعُوا اللَّهَ وَالرَّسُولَ﴾[٤١] [آل عمران: ٣٢] فقَرَنَ طاعته بطاعته رغماً لهم.

١٤م- وقد اختلف المفسرون في معنى قوله تعالىٰ في أمِّ الكتاب: ﴿اهْدِنَا الصِّرَاطَ الْمُسْتَقِيمَ (٦) صِرَاطَ الَّذِينَ أَنْعَمْتَ عَلَيْهِمْ﴾ [الفاتحة: ٦، ٧] فقال أبو العالية[٤٢]،والحسن البَصْري: ﴿الصِّرَاطَ الْمُسْتَقِيمَ﴾ هو رسول الله ﷺ، وخِيار أهل بيته، وأصحابه؛ حكاه عنهما (٢/٦) أبو الحسن الماوَرْدِيُّ، وحكى مكيٌّ[٤٣] عنهما نحوه؛ وقال: هو رسول الله ﷺ وصاحِباه: أبو بكر وعمر رَضِيَ اللَّهُ عَنْهُمَا[٤٤].

وحكىٰ أبو اللَّيث السَّمَرْقَندي مثلَه، عن أبي العالية، في قوله [تعالى]: ﴿صِرَاطَ الَّذِينَ أَنْعَمْتَ عَلَيْهِمْ﴾؛ قال: فبلغَ ذلك الحسَنَ؛ فقال: صدقَ واللهِ! ونَصَح. وحكىٰ الماوَرْدِي ذلك في تفسير: ﴿صِرَاطَ الَّذِينَ أَنْعَمْتَ عَلَيْهِمْ﴾، عن عبد الرحمن بن زَيْد[٤٥].

---

(٤٠) على هامش الأصل مانصه: «الحنان: العطف والرحمة والبركة، ومرَّ ورقة بن نوفل ببلالٍ وهو يعذب فقال: والله! لَئِن قتلتموه لأتخذنَّه حناناً: أي لأتمسَّحنَّ به».

(٤١) نسبه السيوطي في المناهل (١٩) إلى ابن المنذر بنحوه عن مجاهد وقتادة.

(٤٢) هو رُفَيْع بن مِهران الرياحي. تابعي جليل مات سنة (٩٠) أو (٩٣) هـ (التقريب).

(٤٣) هو مكِّيُّ بن أبي طالب، علَّامة مقريء. توفي سنة (٤٣٧ هـ) انظر ترجمته في سير أعلام النبلاء ٥٩١/١٧.

(٤٤) قال السيوطي في المناهل (٢٠): «أخرجه بلفظ مَكِّيٍّ ابنُ جرير وابن أبي حاتم، ثم أخرجه في المستدرك (٢٥٩/٢) من رواية أبي العالية، عن ابن عباس وصححهُ».

(٤٥) هو عبد الرحمن بن زيد بن أسلم. قال الذهبي: كان صاحب قرآن وتفسير. توفي سنة (١٨٢) هـ انظر ترجمته

There are several interpretations of the "firmest, unfailing hand-hold" in the words of Allah Exalted: "...has certainly grasped the firmest, unfailing hand-hold. And Allah is All-Hearing, All-Knowing."[77] Abū 'Abd al-Raḥmān al-Sulamī reported from some scholars that it is Muhammad ﷺ. Others said the "hand-hold" is Islam, or the attestation to the Oneness of Allah ﷻ. Sahl understood the words of Allah Exalted: "If you tried to count Allah's Blessings, you would never be able to number them"[78] to refer to His Blessings upon Muhammad ﷺ. Allah Exalted said: "And the one who has brought the truth and those who embrace it – it is they who are the righteous. They will have whatever they desire with their Lord. That is the reward of the good-doers."[79] Most scholars of *tafsīr* agree that "the one who has brought the truth"[80] refers to Muhammad ﷺ. An alternative opinion suggests that it is the second part of the verse, "those who embrace it [*ṣaddaqa bihī*]", which refers to the Prophet ﷺ. The scholars holding this opinion highlight an alternative recitation of "*ṣaddaqa bihī*" as "*ṣadaqa bihī*", without the *shaddah* on the *dāl*, giving the meaning of "the one who confirms [the truth]". Others stated that "those who embrace it" refers to all believers. Allah Exalted revealed: "Surely in the remembrance of Allah do hearts find comfort."[81] Mujāhid[82] commented, in his explanation of the verse: "[By remembering] Muhammad ﷺ and his companions."

---

77 *al-Baqarah*, 256.

78 *al-Naḥl*, 18.

79 *al-Zumar*, 33-34.

80 *al-Zumar*, 33.

81 *al-Ra'd*, 28.

82 Mujāhid ibn Jabr, leading scholar of the Qur'an. He died, whilst in *sujūd* (prostration), in 102 AH. See *Siyar A'lām al-Nubalā'* (4/449).

وحكىٰ أبو عَبْدِ الرحمن السُّلَمِيّ، عن بعضهم، في تفسير قوله تعالى: ﴿فَقَدِ اسْتَمْسَكَ بِالْعُرْوَةِ الْوُثْقَىٰ لَا انفِصَامَ لَهَا ۗ وَاللَّهُ سَمِيعٌ عَلِيمٌ﴾ [البقرة: ٢٥٦] أنه محمد عليه السلام.

وقيل: الإسلام. وقيل شهادة التوحيد. وقال سَهْلٌ في قوله تعالى: ﴿وَإِن تَعُدُّوا نِعْمَةَ اللَّهِ لَا تُحْصُوهَا﴾ [النحل: ١٨] قال: نعمتُه بمحمد عليه السلام. وقال تعالى: ﴿وَالَّذِي جَاءَ بِالصِّدْقِ وَصَدَّقَ بِهِ ۙ أُولَٰئِكَ هُمُ الْمُتَّقُونَ (٣٣) لَهُم مَّا يَشَاءُونَ عِندَ رَبِّهِمْ ۚ ذَٰلِكَ جَزَاءُ الْمُحْسِنِينَ﴾ [الزمر: ٣٣، ٣٤].

أكثَرُ المفسرين علىٰ أن الذي جاء بالصِّدق هو محمد ﷺ. وقال بعضُهم: وهو الذي صدَّق به. وقرئ: صَدَق، بالتخفيف. وقال غيرهم: الذي صدَّق به المؤمنون. وقيل: أبو بكرٍ. وقيل عليٌّ. وقيل غير هذا من الأقوال.

١٥- وعن مُجاهِدٍ(٤٦) في قوله تعالىٰ: ﴿أَلَا بِذِكْرِ اللَّهِ تَطْمَئِنُّ الْقُلُوبُ﴾ [الرعد: ٢٨] قال: بمحمد ﷺ وأصحابه(٤٧).

في سير أعلام النبلاء ٣٤٩/٨.

(٤٦) هو مجاهد بن جبر، شيخ القراء والمفسرين. مات وهو ساجد سنة (١٠٢) هـ انظر ترجمته في سير أعلام النبلاء (٤٤٩/٤).

(٤٧) نسبه السيوطي في المناهل (٢١) إلى ابن أبي حاتم وابن جرير.

Allah Exalted Describing the Prophet ﷺ as "A Witness", & the Praise & Honour That Implies

Allah Exalted said: "O Prophet! We have sent you as a witness, and a deliverer of good news, and a warner, and a caller to [the Way of] Allah by His Command, and a beacon of light."[83]

In this verse, Allah Exalted establishes the honourable status of the Prophet ﷺ and describes many of his praiseworthy characteristics. He makes the Prophet ﷺ "a witness"[84] over his nation, on account of his delivery of the Divine Message, which is a quality that is unique to him. He is a "deliverer of good news"[85] to those who obey, and a "warner"[86] to those who reject the truth. The Prophet is a "caller"[87] to the worship of, and unadulterated belief in, Allah Exalted without partners, and a "beacon of light"[88] through which people are guided to the truth.

Sheikh Abū Muhammad ibn ʿAttāb ﷺ narrated: "Abū al-Qāsim Ḥātim ibn Muhammad narrated, from Abū al-Ḥasan al-Qābisī, from Abū Zayd al-Marwazī, from Abū ʿAbdullāh Muhammad ibn Yūsuf, from Bukhārī, from Muhammad ibn Sinān, from Fulayḥ, from Hilāl, from ʿAṭā' ibn Yasār, who said: 'I met ʿAbdullāh ibn ʿAmr ibn al-ʿĀṣ, and I said to him: "Tell me about the character of the Messenger of Allah ﷺ." He said: "I swear by Allah, he was described in Torah with some of the same characteristics that appear in the Qur'an. It says:

---

83 *al-Aḥzāb*, 45-46.

84 *al-Aḥzāb*, 45.

85 ibid.

86 ibid.

87 *al-Aḥzāb*, 46.

88 ibid.

الفصل الثاني

فِيْ وصْفِهِ لَهُ تَعالىٰ بالشَّهادَةِ وما يَتَعَلَّقُ بِها مِنَ الثَّنَاءِ والْكَرَامَةِ

قال الله تعالى: ﴿يَا أَيُّهَا النَّبِيُّ إِنَّا أَرْسَلْنَاكَ شَاهِدًا وَمُبَشِّرًا وَنَذِيرًا (٤٥) وَدَاعِيًا إِلَى اللَّهِ بِإِذْنِهِ وَسِرَاجًا مُّنِيرًا﴾ [الأحزاب: ٤٥، ٤٦].

جمع الله تعالى في هذه الآية ضُروباً من رُتَب الأُثْرَةِ[٤٨]، وجُمْلَةَ أوصاف من المِدْحة؛ فجعله شاهداً على أُمَّته لِنَفْسِه بإبلاغهم الرِّسالة، وهي من خصائصه عليه السلام ومُبَشراً لأهلِ طاعته؛ ونَذِيراً لأهل معصيته، وداعِياً إلى توحيده وعبادته؛ وسِرَاجاً مُنيراً يُهتَدىٰ به لِلْحَقِّ.

١٦- حدثنا الشيخ أبو محمد بن عتّاب [رحمه الله] قال: حدثنا أبو القاسم حاتم بن محمد، حدثنا أبو الحسن القابِسيُّ، حدثنا أبو زَيدٍ المَرْوزيُّ، حدثنا أبو عَبْد اللهِ: محمد بن يوسف/ حدثنا البخاري (٧/أ)، حدثنا محمد بن سِنان، حدثنا فُلَيْح، حدثنا هلال، عن عطاء بن يَسَار، قال: لَقِيتُ عَبْدَ اللهِ بن عَمْرو بن العاص، قلتُ: أَخْبِرْني عن صِفَةِ رسولِ الله صلى الله عليه وسلم؟ قال: أَجَل، واللهِ! إنه لموصوفٌ في التَّوْرَاة ببعض صفته في القرآن: ﴿يَا أَيُّهَا النَّبِيُّ إِنَّا أَرْسَلْنَاكَ شَاهِدًا وَمُبَشِّرًا وَنَذِيرًا﴾ [الأحزاب: ٤٥]، وحِرْزاً لِلأُمِّيِّينَ، أَنْتَ عَبْدِي ورسولي، سمَّيتُك المتوكِّلَ، ليس بفَظّ، ولا

---

(٤٨) الأُثْرَةُ: المكرمة المتوارثة.

'O Prophet! We have sent you as a witness, and a deliverer of good news, and a warner.[89] [And we sent you as] a refuge for the illiterate. You are My slave and Messenger, and I have named you al-Mutawakkil[90]. You are not harsh or hard-hearted, neither do you shout in the markets. You do not repay evil with evil. Rather, you overlook and forgive. Allah will not take your soul until this crooked nation has been straightened, and they say "There is no-one worthy of worship except Allah." Through which, the eyes of the blind, the ears of the deaf, and the hearts of the ignorant will be opened."'[91]

Similar descriptions from the Torah were reported from 'Abdullāh ibn Salām[92] and Ka'b al-Aḥbār[93].

In some of the transmissions from Ibn Isḥāq, it also includes: "He does not shout in the markets or use obscene language. I will bless him with every beautiful and noble characteristic. I will make tranquillity his garment, righteousness his motto, piety his essence, wisdom his understanding, honesty and trustworthiness his nature, forgiveness and kindness his character, justice his path, the truth his law, guidance his imam, Islam his religion, and Aḥmad his name. Through him, I will guide the misguided and educate the ignorant."[94]

In another hadith, the Messenger of Allah ﷺ himself informed us of how Allah defined him in the Torah: "My slave, Aḥmad, al-Mukhtār[95], born in Makkah, who will emigrate to Madinah[96]. His

---

89 This sentence is also found in the Qur'an: *al-Aḥzāb*, 45.

90 Meaning, "the one who relies [on Allah]".

91 Reported here from the chain of Bukhārī (2125).

92 Reported by Bukhārī at the end of (2125). Ibn Ḥajar said in *Fatḥ al-Bārī* (4/343): "This chain was connected by Dārimī in his *Musnad* (6), Ya'qūb ibn Sufyān in his *Tārīkh*, and Ṭabarānī."

93 Reported by Aḥmad (2/174) in an authentic narration.

94 Suyūṭī said in *Al-Manāhil*, p.25: "It was reported by Ibn Abī Ḥātim, in his *tafsīr* of Surah al-Fatḥ, from Wahb ibn Munabbih." See also, *Majma' al-Zawā'id* (8/271).

95 Meaning, "the Chosen One".

96 Or he said: "Ṭayyibah".

غليظ، ولا صَخَّاب في الأسواق، ولا يدفَعُ بالسيئةِ السيئةَ، ولكن يَعْفُو ويَغْفِر، ولن يَقْبِضَهُ اللهُ حتى يُقيمَ بهِ المِلَّةَ العَوجَاء، بأَنْ يقولوا: لا إله إلا اللهُ، ويَفْتَحَ به أَعيُناً عُمياً، وآذاناً صُمّاً، وقلوباً غُلْفاً.

١٧- وذُكِر مثلُه عن عبد اللهِ بن سَلَام(٤٩).

١٨- وكَعْبِ الأحبار(٥٠).

١٩- وفي بعضِ طُرُقِهِ عن ابن إسحاق: ولا صَخِبٍ في الأسواق، ولا مُتَزَيِّنٍ بالفُحْش، ولا قَوَّال للخَنَا؛ أُسَدِّدُه لكل جميل، وأَهَبُ له كلَّ خلق كريم، وأجعلُ السكينةَ لباسَه، والبِرَّ شِعَارَه، والتَّقْوَى ضَمِيرَه، والحكمةَ مَعْقولَهُ، والصدقَ والوفاءَ طبيعتَه، والعفوَ والمعروفَ خُلُقَه، والعَدْلَ سيرتَه، والحقَّ شريَعَتَهُ، والهدَى إمامَهُ، والإسلامَ مِلَّتَه، وأَحْمَد اسْمَه، أهدي به بعد الضلالةِ، وأُعَلِّم به بعد الجَهالة، وأرفعُ به بعد الخَمَالَةِ، وأُسَمِّي به بعد النُّكْرة، وأُكثِّرُ به بعد القِلَّة، وأُغني به بعد العَيْلَةِ، وأجمعُ به بعد الفُرْقَة، وأُؤَلِّف به بينَ قُلوبٍ مختلفةٍ، وأهواءٍ متشتِّتةٍ، وأُممٍ مُتَفَرِّقة، وأَجعل أُمَّتَهُ خيرَ أُمةٍ أُخْرِجَتْ للناس(٥١).

٢٠- وفي حديث آخر: أَخبرنا رسولُ الله ﷺ عن صِفته في التَّوْراة:

---

(٤٩) أخرجه البخاري تعليقاً (٢١٢٥). قال الحافظ في الفتح (٣٤٣/٤): «وطريقه هذه وصلها الدارمي في مسنده برقم (٦)، ويعقوب بن سفيان في تاريخه والطبراني، جميعاً، بإسناد واحدٍ عنه». وسيعيده المصنف برقم (٢١٢).

(٥٠) حديث كعب الأحبار أخرجه أحمد ١٧٤/٢، وهو حديث صحيح.

(٥١) قال في المناهل (٢٥): «أخرجه ابن أبي حاتم في تفسير سورة الفتح عن وهب بن مُنَبِّه». وانظر مجمع الزوائد ٢٧١/٨. (الخنا): الفول الفاحش. (العَيْلَة): الفقر. (الخمالة): يقال خمل ذكره: خفي.

nation are the ones who praise Allah no matter the circumstances."[97]

Allah Exalted said: "[They are] the ones who follow the Messenger, the unlettered Prophet, whose description they find in their Torah and the Gospel. He commands them to do good and forbids them from evil, permits for them what is lawful and forbids to them what is impure, and relieves them from their burdens and the shackles that bound them. [Only] those who believe in him, honour and support him, and follow the light sent down to him will be successful. Say, [O Prophet,] 'O humanity! I am Allah's Messenger to you all. To Him [alone] belongs the kingdom of the heavens and the earth. There is no god [worthy of worship] except Him. He gives life and causes death.' So believe in Allah and His Messenger, the unlettered Prophet, who believes in Allah and His Revelations. And follow him, so you may be [rightly] guided."[98]

And: "It is out of Allah's mercy that you [O Prophet] have been lenient with them. Had you been cruel or hard-hearted, they would have certainly abandoned you. So pardon them, ask Allah's Forgiveness for them, and consult with them in [conducting] matters. Once you make a decision, put your trust in Allah. Surely Allah loves those who trust in Him."[99]

Al-Samarqandī commented: "Allah reminded the believers of His Favour in making the Prophet ﷺ merciful, compassionate, and lenient towards them. Had the Prophet ﷺ been harshly-spoken, they would have abandoned him, but Allah Exalted endowed him with an easygoing, gentle, and charitable personality." Al-Ḍaḥḥāk[100] said

---

97 Reported by Haythamī in *Majma' al-Zawā'id* (8/271) from Ibn Mas'ūd. Haythamī said: "It was related by Ṭabarānī, and the chain contains narrators I do not know." Suyūṭī traced the hadith in *Al-Manāhil*, p. 26, to Abū Nu'aym in *Al-Dalā'il*. See also Dārimī (1/4-6).

98 *al-A'rāf*, 157-158.

99 Āl 'Imrān, 159.

100 Al-Ḍaḥḥāk ibn Muzāḥim, a fountain of knowledge from among the Followers. He died in 100 AH. See *Siyar A'lām al-Nubalā'* (4/598).

«عَبْدِي أَحْمَدُ المختارُ، مَوْلدهُ بمكةَ، ومُهاجَرُه بالمدينة - أو قال: طَيْبة - أُمّتُهُ الحَمّادون لله على كلّ حال»(٥٢).

وقال تعالى: ﴿الَّذِينَ يَتَّبِعُونَ الرَّسُولَ النَّبِيَّ الْأُمِّيَّ الَّذِي يَجِدُونَهُ مَكْتُوبًا عِندَهُمْ فِي التَّوْرَاةِ وَالْإِنجِيلِ يَأْمُرُهُم بِالْمَعْرُوفِ وَيَنْهَاهُمْ عَنِ الْمُنكَرِ وَيُحِلُّ لَهُمُ الطَّيِّبَاتِ وَيُحَرِّمُ عَلَيْهِمُ الْخَبَائِثَ وَيَضَعُ عَنْهُمْ إِصْرَهُمْ وَالْأَغْلَالَ الَّتِي كَانَتْ عَلَيْهِمْ ۚ فَالَّذِينَ آمَنُوا بِهِ وَعَزَّرُوهُ وَنَصَرُوهُ وَاتَّبَعُوا النُّورَ الَّذِي أُنزِلَ مَعَهُ ۙ أُولَٰئِكَ هُمُ الْمُفْلِحُونَ (١٥٧) قُلْ يَا أَيُّهَا النَّاسُ إِنِّي رَسُولُ اللَّهِ إِلَيْكُمْ جَمِيعًا الَّذِي لَهُ مُلْكُ السَّمَاوَاتِ وَالْأَرْضِ ۖ لَا إِلَٰهَ إِلَّا هُوَ يُحْيِي وَيُمِيتُ ۖ فَآمِنُوا بِاللَّهِ وَرَسُولِهِ النَّبِيِّ الْأُمِّيِّ الَّذِي يُؤْمِنُ بِاللَّهِ وَكَلِمَاتِهِ وَاتَّبِعُوهُ لَعَلَّكُمْ تَهْتَدُونَ﴾ [الأعراف: ١٥٧، ١٥٨]. وقال تعالى: ﴿فَبِمَا رَحْمَةٍ مِّنَ اللَّهِ لِنتَ لَهُمْ ۖ وَلَوْ كُنتَ فَظًّا غَلِيظَ الْقَلْبِ لَانفَضُّوا مِنْ حَوْلِكَ ۖ فَاعْفُ عَنْهُمْ وَاسْتَغْفِرْ لَهُمْ وَشَاوِرْهُمْ فِي الْأَمْرِ ۖ فَإِذَا عَزَمْتَ فَتَوَكَّلْ عَلَى اللَّهِ ۚ إِنَّ اللَّهَ يُحِبُّ الْمُتَوَكِّلِينَ﴾ [آل عمران: ١٥٩].

قال السَّمَرْقَنْديُّ: ذكَّرهم اللهُ مِنَّتَهُ أنه جعل رسوله رحيماً بالمؤمنين، رؤوفاً ليّن الجانبِ، ولو كان فظّاً خَشِناً (٧/ب) في القول لتفرَّقُوا من حوله، ولكن جعله الله [تعالىٰ] سَمْحاً، سَهلاً، طَلْقاً برّاً لطيفاً. هكذا قاله

(٥٢) ذكره الهيثمي في مجمع الزوائد ٢٧١/٨ من حديث ابن مسعود وقال: «رواه الطبراني وفيه من لم أعرفهم». وزاد نسبته السيوطي في المناهل (٢٦) إلى أبي نعيم في الدلائل. وانظر الدارمي ٤/١-٦.

something similar. Allah Exalted said: "And so We have made you [believers] an upright community so that you may be witnesses over humanity and that the Messenger may be a witness over you."[101] Abū al-Ḥasan al-Qābisī[102] observed: "In this verse, Allah elucidates the distinction of the Prophet ﷺ and his nation, as He does when He says: 'and in this [Qur'an], so that the Messenger may be a witness over you, and that you may be witnesses over humanity.'[103]"

Allah describes the nation of the Prophet ﷺ as "an upright [*wasaṭ*] community"[104]. "*Wasaṭ*", literally meaning "middle", implies here that they are the most balanced and just, and the best. Allah Exalted also revealed: "So how will it be when We bring a witness from every faith-community and bring you [O Prophet] as a witness against yours?"[105] Meaning: "Just as we guided you, we have favoured you by making you the best and most equitable nation, both in order for you to serve as witnesses on behalf of the other Prophets ﷺ, and for the Messenger of Allah ﷺ to bear witness to your truthfulness."

It was said that Allah Exalted will ask the Prophets if they relayed the message they were sent with. They will say that they did. Then, their nations will respond: "There has never come to us a deliverer of good news or a warner."[106] The nation of Muhammad ﷺ will bear witness on behalf of the Prophets, and the Messenger of Allah ﷺ will endorse and commend them.[107] Al-Samarqandī said that the verse meant: "You [i.e., the believers] are a proof against all those who op-

---

101 *al-Baqarah*, 143.

102 'Alī ibn Muhammad al-Maghribī, a great imam, *hāfiẓ*, jurist, and leading scholar of his country. He died in Kairouan in 403 AH. See *Siyar A'lām al-Nubalā'* (17/158).

103 *al-Ḥajj*, 78.

104 *al-Baqarah*, 143.

105 *al-Nisā'*, 41.

106 As found in *al-Mā'idah*, 19.

107 This meaning is taken from the hadith of Abū Sa'īd al-Khudrī, reported by Bukhārī (3339).

الضَّحَّاكُ(٥٣). وقال تعالىٰ: ﴿وَكَذَٰلِكَ جَعَلْنَاكُمْ أُمَّةً وَسَطًا لِّتَكُونُوا شُهَدَاءَ عَلَى النَّاسِ وَيَكُونَ الرَّسُولُ عَلَيْكُمْ شَهِيدًا﴾ [البقرة: ١٤٣]. قال أبو الحسَنِ القابسي(٥٤): أَبَانَ اللهُ [تعالىٰ] فَضْلَ نبينا ﷺ، وفَضْلَ أُمتهِ بهذه الآية، وفي قوله في الآية الأخرى: ﴿وَفِي هَٰذَا لِيَكُونَ الرَّسُولُ شَهِيدًا عَلَيْكُمْ وَتَكُونُوا شُهَدَاءَ عَلَى النَّاسِ﴾ [الحج: ٧٨]. وكذلك قوله [تعالى]: ﴿فَكَيْفَ إِذَا جِئْنَا مِنْ كُلِّ أُمَّةٍ بِشَهِيدٍ وَجِئْنَا بِكَ عَلَىٰ هَٰؤُلَاءِ شَهِيدًا﴾[النساء: ٤١] و قوله [تعالى]: وَسَطاً: أي عَدْلاً خِياراً. ومعنى هذه الآية: وكما هدَيْنَاكُم فكذَلكَ خصَصْناكُم وَفَضَّلْناكم بأَنْ جعَلْناكم أمةً خِياراً عدولاً؛ لتشهدوا للأنبياء عليهم السلام على أُمَمِهم، ويشهدَ لكم الرسولُ بالصِّدْق.

٢١- [و] قيل: إنّ اللهَ جلَّ جلالهُ إذا سأل الأنبياءَ: هل بلَّغْتُم؟ فيقولون: نَعَمْ: فتقول أُمَمُهُم: ما جاءنا مِنْ بشيرٍ ولا نَذيرٍ؛ فتشهد أمّةُ محمدٍ ﷺ للأنبياء(٥٥)؛ ويُزَكّيهم النبيُّ ﷺ(٥٦). وقيل: معنى الآية: إنكم حُجّةٌ على كلِّ مَنْ خالفكم، والرسولُ حجّةٌ عليكم. حكاه السَّمَرْقندي. وقال [الله] تعالى: ﴿وَبَشِّرِ الَّذِينَ آمَنُوا أَنَّ لَهُمْ قَدَمَ صِدْقٍ عِنْدَ رَبِّهِمْ﴾ [يونس: ٢].

---

(٥٣) الضَّحَّاك: هو ابن مزاحم، تابعي من أوعية العلم مات بعد سنة (١٠٠ هـ). انظر سير أعلام النبلاء ٥٩٨/٤.

(٥٤) هو الإمام الحافظ الفقيه، عالم المغرب: علي بن محمد المعافري. مات بمدينة القيروان سنة (٤٠٣ هـ). انظر ترجمته في سير أعلام النبلاء ١٥٨/١٧.

(٥٥) على هامش الأصل زيادة: «عليهم» وهي ليست في المطبوع.

(٥٦) هذا المعنى جاء في حديث أبي سعيد الخدري عند البخاري (٣٣٣٩).

pose you, and the Prophet ﷺ is a proof against you." Allah Exalted said: "And give good news to the believers that they will have an honourable status with their Lord."[108] Qatādah, al-Ḥasan al-Baṣrī, and Zayd ibn Aslam[109] said: "an honourable status"[110] refers to the intercession of Muhammad ﷺ on the believers' behalf. Al-Ḥasan al-Baṣrī also said: "It is the blessing of being sent the Prophet ﷺ." Abū Sa'īd al-Khudrī ﷺ commented: "It is the intercession of their Prophet ﷺ. He is an honourable intercessor in the sight of their Lord."

Sahl ibn 'Abdullāh al-Tustarī observed: "It is the Mercy Allah Exalted had already placed in Muhammad ﷺ."

Al-Sulamī related, from Muhammad ibn 'Alī al-Tirmidhī[111]: "Muhammad ﷺ is the imam of the people of truth, and the one whose intercession is accepted and whose questions are answered."

---

108 *Yūnus*, 2.

109 Abū 'Abdullāh al-'Adawī, a great scholar, jurist, and role model. He passed away in 136 AH. See *Siyar A'lām al-Nubalā'* (5/316).

110 *Yūnus*, 2.

111 Also known as al-Ḥakīm al-Tirmidhī. He was the author of *Nawādir al-Uṣūl*. Not to be confused with Tirmidhī, author of *Al-Jāmi' al-Ṣaḥīḥ*. Dhahabī said: "He is a man of wisdom, exhortation, and radiance. If only it were not for his mistakes [in narrating hadiths]." He died in approximately 320 AH. See *Siyar A'lām al-Nubalā'* (13/439).

قال قَتادة، والحسَن، وزَيْد بن أسلم(٥٧): ﴿قَدَمَ صِدْقٍ﴾: هو محمدٌ ﷺ، يشفَعُ لهم. وعن الحسَن أيضاً قال: هي مصيبتُهم بنبيِّهم. وعن أبي سَعِيد الخُدْري [رَضِيَ اللهُ عَنْهُ]: هي شفاعةُ نبيِّهم محمدٍ ﷺ؛ هو شفيعُ صِدْقٍ عنْدَ ربهم. وقال سَهْلُ بن عبد اللهِ التُّسْتَرِيُّ: هي سابقةُ رحمةٍ أودعها [اللّٰه] في محمد ﷺ. وقال محمد بن علي التِّرْمِذِيُّ(٥٨): هو إمامُ الصادقين والصدِّيقين، الشفيعُ المُطَاع، والسائلُ المُجابُ، محمدٌ ﷺ، حكاه عنه السُّلَمِيُّ.

---

(٥٧) هو الإمام الحجة القدوة، أبو عبد الله العدوي الفقيه. مات سنة (١٣٦ هـ). انظر ترجمته في سير أعلام النبلاء ٥/٣١٦.

(٥٨) هو المعروف بالحكيم الترمذي صاحب «نوادر الأصول». وهو غير الترمذي صاحب الجامع الصحيح. قال الحافظ الذهبي: «له حكم ومواعظ وجلالة، لولا هفوة بدت منه». مات نحو سنة (٣٢٠ هـ). انظر ترجمته في سير أعلام النبلاء ١٣/٤٣٩.

The Kindness of Allah Exalted When He Addresses The Prophet ﷺ

Allah Exalted employs a gentle tone when addressing His beloved Prophet ﷺ. For example, He says: "May Allah pardon you [O Prophet]! Why did you give them permission [to stay behind]?"[112] Makkī said: "[Allah Exalted] begins his statement in the manner of: 'May Allah rectify your affairs and elevate your position.'" 'Awn ibn 'Abdullāh[113] commented: "Allah informed the Prophet ﷺ of His Pardon for him before mentioning his mistake." Al-Samarqandī related another interpretation of the verse: "May Allah bless you, O you with the pure heart! Why did you give them permission?" He continued: "If Allah Exalted had begun with 'Why did you give them permission?'[114], then perhaps the heart of the Prophet ﷺ would have burst open with fear. Instead, out of His Mercy, Allah informed the Prophet ﷺ of His Pardon first, so that his heart would remain calm. Then, He said: 'Why did you give them permission before clarifying who had a genuine excuse and who was lying?'" Such an example of the high status of the Prophet ﷺ in the sight of his Lord b is evident to any person of understanding. Understanding the true extent of His Love and Mercy towards him would be enough to sever arteries.

Nifṭawayh[115] said: "Some people think that the Prophet ﷺ was reprimanded in this verse. Far from it! In reality, the Prophet ﷺ was

112 *al-Tawbah*, 43.

113 Abū 'Abdullāh al-Hudhalī, a great role model and devout worshipper. He died in the 110s AH. See *Siyar A'lām al-Nubalā'* (5/103).

114 *al-Tawbah*, 43.

115 Ibrāhīm ibn Muhammad, the knowledgeable grammarian and scholar. He was born in 244 AH and passed away in 323 AH. See *Siyar A'lām al-Nubalā'* (15/75).

الفصل الثالث

فِيمَا وَرَدَ فِي(٥٩) خِطَابِهِ إِيَّاهُ مَوْرِدَ المُلَاطَفَةِ والمَبَرَّةِ

من ذلك قوله تعالى: ﴿عَفَا اللَّهُ عَنكَ لِمَ أَذِنتَ لَهُمْ﴾ [التوبة: ٤٣].

قال أبو محمد: مَكِّيٌّ: قيل: هذا افتتاح كلامٍ بمنزلة: أصلحكَ الله، وأعزَّك الله (٨/أ). وقال عَون بن عبد الله(٦٠): أخبره بالعَفْو قبل أنْ يُخْبِره بالذَّنْبِ.

[و] حكى السَّمَرْقَنْدِي عن بعضهم أنَّ معناه: عافاكَ اللهُ، يا سليم القلبِ! لِمَ أذِنْتَ لهم؟. قال: ولو بدأ النبيَّ ﷺ بقوله: ﴿لِمَ أَذِنتَ لَهُمْ﴾ لخِيفَ عليه أنْ يَنْشقَّ قلبهُ من هيبةِ هذا الكلامِ، لكنَّ الله تعالى برحمته أَخبره بالعفو حتى سكن قَلْبُه، ثم قال له: لم أَذِنْتَ لهم بالتخلف حتى يتبيَّنَ لك الصادقُ في عُذْرِه من الكاذب؟ وفي هذا منْ عظِيم منزلته عند الله ما لا يَخْفى على ذي لُبٍّ. ومن إكرامه إياه وبرّه به ما ينقطِعُ - دون معرفةِ غايتِهِ - نِيَاطُ القَلْبِ(٦١). قال نِفْطَوَيْه(٦٢): ذهب ناسٌ إلى أنَّ النبيَّ صلى الله عليه وسلم

---

(٥٩) في المطبوع: «من».

(٦٠) هو الإمام القدوة العابد: أبو عبد الله الهذلي. توفي سنة بضع عشرة ومئة للهجرة. انظر ترجمته في سير أعلام النبلاء ١٠٣/٥.

(٦١) نياط: عرق غليظ عُلِّق به القلب إلى الرئتين (المعجم الوسيط). وعلى هامش الأصل: «النياط: عرق غُلِّف به القلب».

(٦٢) هو الإمام الحافظ النحوي العلامة الإخباري إبراهيم بن محمد. ولد سنة (٢٤٤ هـ) ومات في سنة (٣٢٣ هـ). انظر ترجمته في سير أعلام النبلاء ٧٥/١٥.

being commended. Allah Exalted informed the Prophet ﷺ that even if he had not excused the hypocrites [from joining the Muslims in preparing and leaving for battle] they would have stayed behind anyway, so there was no blame in excusing them."

For every Muslim who struggles against their own desires and holds fast to the boundaries established by Allah Exalted, it is incumbent upon them to adopt the manner of the Qur'an in their speech and actions, and their interactions with others, for that is the essence of true knowledge and the pinnacle of good character in both religious and worldly affairs. Let him ponder the sublime Grace of the Lord of lords, the Beneficient over all, the One free of need, when He began with honouring [the Prophet ﷺ] before reminding, and chose to mention His Pardon before any mistake of the Prophet ﷺ, if there had been a mistake in the first place. Allah Exalted said: "Had We not made you steadfast, you probably would have inclined to them a little."[116] Some scholars observed that whereas Allah Exalted censured other Prophets after they had made mistakes, He addressed our Prophet ﷺ before any mistake had been made. In this way, He shows the greatest degree of care and attention for him. Observe how Allah Exalted mentions the resolve and integrity of the Prophet ﷺ before mentioning a trait that would be disliked. Allah Exalted did not wish His Prophet ﷺ to fixate on the latter, but by addressing him in such a manner, the innocence and honour of the Prophet ﷺ are firmly upheld. Allah Exalted revealed: "We certainly know that what they say grieves you [O Prophet]. It is not your honesty they question – it is Allah's signs that the wrongdoers deny."[117]

'Alī ﷺ narrated: "Abū Jahl said to the Prophet ﷺ: 'We are not rejecting you; rather, we are rejecting [the message] you have brought.'

116 *al-Isrā'*, 74.
117 *al-An'ām*, 33.

مُعَاتَبٌ بهذه الآية، وحاشَاهُ من ذلك، بل كان مُخَيَّراً فلما أذِنَ لهم أعلمه اللهُ [تعالى] أنه لو لَمْ يَأْذَنْ لهم لقَعَدُوا لِنفاقِهم، وأنه لا حَرجَ عليه في الإذْنِ لهم. قال القاضي أبو الفضل - رحمه الله - : يجبُ على المسلم المجاهِدِ نَفْسَهُ، الرائضِ(٦٣) بِزمام الشريعةِ خُلُقَه، أَن يتأَدَّبَ بأَدَبِ القرآن في قوله وفعْله، ومعُاطاتِه ومُحَاوراته، فهو عُنْصُرُ المعارف الحقيقيةِ، وروضةُ الآداب الدينية والدُّنْيَوية، ولْيتأَمَّل هذه الملاطفة العجيبةَ في السؤال من رَبِّ الأرباب، المُنْعِم على الكلِّ، المُسْتَغْني عن الجميع، ويَسْتثيرُ(٦٤) ما فيها من الفوائد،وكيف ابتدأ بالإكرامِ قبل العَتْبِ، وآنَسَ بالعفو قبل ذكْرِ الذنب، إنْ كان ثَمَّ ذَنْبٌ. وقال تعالى: ﴿وَلَوْلَا أَن ثَبَّتْنَاكَ لَقَدْ كِدتَّ تَرْكَنُ إِلَيْهِمْ شَيْئًا قَلِيلًا﴾ [الإسراء: ٧٤]. قال بعضُ المتكلمين: عاتَبَ اللهُ [تعالى] الأنبياءَ [عليهم السلام] بَعْدَ الزَّلَّاتِ، وعاتب نبيَّنا عليه السلام قبل وُقُوعِه، ليكونَ بذلك أشدَّ انتهاءً ومحافظةً لشرائطِ المَحبَّةِ، وهذه غايةُ العِنايةِ. ثم انْظُر كيف بدأ بثَباتِه وسلامتهِ قبل ذِكْرِ ما عَتَبه عليه وخِيفَ أنْ يَرْكَنَ إليه، ففي أثناءِ عَتْبِه براءتُه، وفي طيِّ (٨/ب) تَخْويفِهِ تَأْمينهُ وكرامتهُ. ومثله قولهُ تعالى: ﴿قَدْ نَعْلَمُ إِنَّهُ لَيَحْزُنُكَ الَّذِى يَقُولُونَ فَإِنَّهُمْ لَا يُكَذِّبُونَكَ وَلَكِنَّ الظَّالِمِينَ بِآيَاتِ اللَّهِ يَجْحَدُونَ﴾ [الأنعام: ٣٣].

٢٢- قال عليّ رضيَ اللهُ عنهُ: قال أبو جهل للنبي ﷺ: إنّا لا نُكذِّبُكَ

---

(٦٣) المذلِّل.

(٦٤) يستثيرُ: يظهر. وفي المطبوع: «وَيَسْتَتر».

So, Allah Exalted revealed: 'It is not your honesty they question – it is Allah's signs that the wrongdoers deny.'[118]"[119] It was related that the Prophet ﷺ would become sad when his people denied him. Jibrīl ﷺ came to him and said: "What is making you sad?" The Prophet ﷺ answered: "My people have rejected me." Jibrīl ﷺ replied: "Certainly, they do not know that you are honest and sincere", and then Allah Exalted revealed the verse.[120] In this verse, Allah Exalted consoles the Prophet ﷺ by confirming that even those who reject his message know that he is truthful. Before Prophethood, they would call him "the Trustworthy"[121]. These reassurances drove away the hurt and worry the Prophet ﷺ felt at being branded a liar. Then, Allah Exalted named those who had slandered the Prophet ﷺ as oppressors and deniers of the truth, saying: "it is Allah's Signs that the wrongdoers deny."[122] He absolves the Prophet ﷺ of any shame or disgrace, and condemns those who refuse to accept the truth – the epitome of oppression – as being hamstrung by their own stubbornness. To "deny" in this context refers to those who know the truth and then reject it anyway. As Allah Exalted says in another verse: "And, although their hearts were convinced the signs were true, they still denied them wrongfully and arrogantly."[123] After consoling the Prophet ﷺ, Allah Exalted offers further encouragement through a reminder of those who preceded him, and promises victory: "Indeed, Messengers before you were rejected but patiently endured rejection and persecution until Our Help came to them. And Allah's Promise [to help] is

118 ibid.

119 Reported by Tirmidhī (3064). Authenticated by Ḥākim in *Al-Mustadrak* (2/315) and Aḥmad Shākir in 'Umdat *al-Tafsīr* (5/25).

120 Suyūṭī said in *Al-Manāhil*, p. 33: "I did not find this narration."

121 "al-Amīn".

122 *al-An'ām*, 33.

123 *al-Naml*, 14.

ولكن نُكذِّبُ ما جِئْتَ به، فأنزل الله تعالى: ﴿فَإِنَّهُمْ لَا يُكَذِّبُونَكَ وَلَٰكِنَّ الظَّالِمِينَ بِآيَاتِ اللَّهِ يَجْحَدُونَ﴾[٦٥] [الأنعام: ٣٣].

٢٣- ورُوِي أنَّ النبيَّ ﷺ لما كذّبه قومُه حَزِن، فجاءه جبريلُ عليه السلام فقال: ما يُحْزِنُك؟ قال: «كَذَّبَنِي قَوْمِي» فقال: إنهم يَعْلمون أنكَ صادِق، فأنزل الله [تعالى] الآية[٦٦]. ففي هذه الآيةِ مَنْزَعٌ لطيفُ المأخَذ، مِنْ تَسْليتِه تعالى له عليه السلام، وإلطافه [به] في القَوْلِ، بأَنْ قَرَّرَ عنده أنه صادقٌ عندهم، وأنَّهم غيْرُ مكذِّبين له، مُعْتَرِفون بصِدْقه قولاً واعتقاداً، وقد كانوا يُسَمُّونه - قَبْل النبوَّة - الأمينَ، فدَفع بهذا التقرير ارْتِماضَ[٦٧] نَفْسه بِسِمَةِ الكذب، ثم جعل[٦٨] الذَّمَّ لهم بتسْمِيتهم جاحِدِينَ ظالمين، فقال الله تعالى: ﴿وَلَٰكِنَّ الظَّالِمِينَ بِآيَاتِ اللَّهِ يَجْحَدُونَ﴾ [الأنعام: ٣٣]. فحاشاه من الوَصْمِ[٦٩]، وطوَّقَهم بالمعاندة بتكذيب الآياتِ حقيقةَ الظُّلْمِ، إذ الجَحْدُ إنما يكون ممَّن علمَ الشيء ثم أنكره، كقوله تعالى: ﴿وَجَحَدُوا بِهَا وَاسْتَيْقَنَتْهَا أَنْفُسُهُمْ ظُلْمًا وَعُلُوًّا﴾ [النمل: ١٤]. ثم عَزَّاه وآنسه بما ذكره عمَّنْ قَبْله، ووعده النصْرَ بقوله [تعالى]: ﴿وَلَقَدْ كُذِّبَتْ رُسُلٌ

---

(٦٥) أخرجه الترمذي (٣٠٦٤)، وصححه الحاكم في المستدرك ٣١٥/٢، والعلامة أحمد شاكر في عمدة التفسير ٢٥/٥. وسيعيده المصنف برقم (٢٨٠)

(٦٦) قال في المناهل (٣٣): «لم أجده».

(٦٧) ارتماض: ارتمض من كذا: اشتد عليه وأقلقه (المعجم الوسيط).

(٦٨) فوقها أثبت الناسخ كلمة: «الرب».

(٦٩) فحاشاه من الوصم: أي نزّهه وبرّأه من العيب والعار.

never broken. And you have already received some of the narratives of these Messengers."[124] In the recitations of Nāfiʿ and al-Kisāʾī, "*lā yukadhdhibūnaka*" (translated above as "It is not your honesty they question"[125]) is read as "*lā yukdhibūnaka*", without the *shaddah* on the *dhāl*. This gives the meaning: "They do not find you to be a liar." Al-Farrāʾ and al-Kisāʾī said the verse meant: "They do not say that you are a liar." Others interpreted the meaning as: "They do not even accuse you of lying, [let alone] prove that to be the case." For those who recited "*lā yukadhdhibūnaka*" with the *shaddah* on the *dhāl*, the meaning is: "They do not complain about you lying" or "They do not believe that you are lying".

From the special characteristics of the Prophet ﷺ, and the immense Love of Allah Exalted for him, He does not address him by his name. Allah Exalted calls all the other Prophets by their given names, saying: "O Adam"[126], "O Nūḥ"[127], "O Ibrāhīm"[128], "O Mūsā"[129], "O Dāwūd"[130], "O ʿĪsā"[131], "O Zakariyyā"[132], and "O Yaḥyā"[133]. But when He addresses Muhammad ﷺ, He says: "O Messenger"[134], "O Prophet"[135], "O you wrapped [in your clothes]"[136], and "O you covered up [in your clothes]"[137].

---

124 *al-Anʿām*, 34.
125 *al-Anʿām*, 33.
126 e.g., *al-Baqarah*, 23.
127 e.g., *Hūd*, 46.
128 e.g., *al-Ṣaffāt*, 104.
129 e.g., *Ṭā Hā*, 11.
130 *Ṣad*, 26.
131 e.g., Āl ʿImrān, 55.
132 *Maryam*, 7.
133 *Maryam*, 12.
134 e.g., *al-Māʾidah*, 41.
135 e.g., *al-Anfāl*, 64.
136 *al-Muzzammil*, 1.
137 *al-Muddaththir*, 1.

مِّن قَبْلِكَ فَصَبَرُوا عَلَىٰ مَا كُذِّبُوا وَأُوذُوا حَتَّىٰ أَتَاهُمْ نَصْرُنَا ۚ وَلَا مُبَدِّلَ لِكَلِمَاتِ اللَّهِ ۚ وَلَقَدْ جَاءَكَ مِن نَّبَإِ الْمُرْسَلِينَ﴾ [الأنعام: ٣٤].

فمَنْ قرأ [لا] ﴿يُكْذِبُونَكَ﴾ بالتخفيف(٧٠)، فمعناه: لا يَجِدونكَ كاذباً. وقال الفَرَّاءُ(٧١)، والكِسَائِيُ(٧٢): لا يقولونَ إنكَ كاذب.

وقيل: لا يَحْتَجُّون على كَذِبك، ولا يُثْبِتُونه.

ومن قرأ بالتشديد فمعناه: لا يَنْسُبُونَك إلىٰ الكذب. وقيل: لا يعتقدون كذبَكَ. ومما ذُكر من خصائصه، وبِرِّ الله تعالى به، أنَّ الله تعالى خاطبَ جميعَ الأنبياء بأسمائهم، فقال تعالى: يا آدم! يا نوح! يا إبراهيم! (٧٣) [يا موسى]! يا داود! يا عيسى! يا زكريا! يا يحيي! ولم يخاطَبْ هو إلاَّ: يا أيُّها الرسولُ! يا أيها النبيُّ! يا أيُّها المُزَّمِّل! يا أيها المُدَّثِّر!

---

(٧٠) هذه قراءة نافع والكسائي (المبسوط في القراءات العشر).

(٧١) هو الإمام العلامة يحي بن زياد الأسدي، النحوي. مات بطريق الحج سنة (٢٠٧ هـ) وله ثلاث وستون سنة. انظر ترجمته في سير أعلام النبلاء ١١٨/١٠.

(٧٢) هو الإمام شيخ القراءة والعربية: علي بن حمزة الأسدي، الملقب بالكسائي، لكساءٍ أحرم فيه، مات سنة (١٨٩ هـ) عن سبعين سنة. انظر ترجمته في سير أعلام النبلاء ١٣١/٩.

(٧٣) قوله: «يا إبراهيم» لم يرد في المطبوع.

Allah Exalted Swearing by the Prestige & Honour of the Prophet ﷺ

Allah Exalted says: "By your life [O Prophet], they certainly wandered blindly, intoxicated [by lust]."[138] The scholars of *tafsīr* agree that in this verse, Allah swears by the length of the life of Muhammad ﷺ. There is no greater honour than this. The word "*'amruka*", translated here as "By your life", has been variously interpreted as "By your remaining", "By your living", and "By your life".

Ibn 'Abbās said: "Allah Exalted did not create or scatter a single soul more beloved and honoured to Him than Muhammad ﷺ, and I did not hear Him swear by anyone's life apart from his." Abū al-Jawzā'[139] said: "Allah did not swear by anyone's life apart from Muhammad ﷺ, because he is the most noble of all creation in His sight."

There is some difference of opinion regarding the meaning of "*Yā Sīn*"[140] at the beginning of the surah: "*Yā Sīn*. By the Qur'an, rich in wisdom!"[141] Makkī relates a narration from the Prophet ﷺ in which he said: "I have ten names with my Lord", and mentioned that "*Ṭā Hā*"[142] and "*Yā Sīn*"[143] were two of those names.[144]

---

138 *al-Ḥijr*, 72.

139 Aws ibn 'Abdullāh al-Baṣrī, a leading scholar and devout worshipper from the Followers. He was killed at the Battle of Dayr al-Jamājim in 83 AH. See *Siyar A'lām al-Nubalā'* (4/371).

140 *Yā Sīn*, 1.

141 *Yā Sīn*, 1-2.

142 *Ṭā Hā*, 1.

143 *Yā Sīn*, 1.

144 Suyūṭī said in *Al-Manāhil*, p. 35: "[Reported by] Abū Nu'aym in *Al-Dalā'il* and Ibn Mardawayh in his *Tafsīr*, from the chain of Abū Yaḥyā al-Taymī (who would fabricate hadiths), from Sayf ibn Wahb (who was a weak narrator), from Abū al-Ṭufayl." Ibn Qayyim al-Jawziyyah said in *Tuḥfat al-Mawdūd*, p. 93: "As for the lay-people who say that '*Yā Sīn*' and '*Ṭā* Hā' are

الفصل الرابع

فِيْ قَسَمِهِ تَعالى بِعَظِيْمِ قَدْرِهِ

قال الله تعالى: ﴿لَعَمْرُكَ إِنَّهُمْ لَفِى سَكْرَتِهِمْ يَعْمَهُونَ﴾ [الحِجْر: ٧٢]. اتَّفق أهْلُ (٩/أ) التفسير في هذا أنه قَسَمٌ من الله - جلَّ جلالهُ - بمُدَّةِ حياةِ محمد ﷺ، وأَصْلُه ضَمُّ العين، مِن العُمُرِ، ولكنها فُتحت لكثرة الاستعمالِ. ومعناه: وبقائكَ! يا محمد! وقيل: وعَيْشِكَ! وقيل: وَحيَاتِكَ!

وهذه نِهَايَةُ التعظيم، وغايةُ البِرِّ والتشريف. قال ابنُ عباس [رَضِيَ اللهُ عَنْهُمَا]: ما خلقَ الله [تعالى]، وما ذرَأَ، وما بَرَأَ نفساً - أكرمَ عليه مِنْ محمد ﷺ، وما سمعتُ الله تعالى أقسم بحياةِ أحدٍ غَيْرِه. وقال أبو الجَوْزَاء[٧٤]: ما أَقْسَمَ الله تعالى بحياةِ أحدٍ غيْرِ محمدٍ ﷺ؛ لأنه أَكْرَمُ البريَّةِ عنده.

وقال تعالى: ﴿يس (١) وَالْقُرْآنِ الْحَكِيمِ﴾ الآيات [يس: ١، ٢].

اختلف المُفَسِّرون في معنى ﴿يس﴾ على أقوال:

٢٤- فحكى أبو محمد، مَكِّيٌّ: أنه رُوي عن النبي ﷺ أ[أنه] قال: «لي عند رَبِّي عَشَرَةُ أسماءٍ» ذكر أَنَّ منها: ﴿طه﴾ و ﴿يس﴾، اسمانِ له[٧٥].

---

(٧٤) هو أوس بن عبد الله البصري، تابعي من كبار العلماء والعباد. قتل يوم الجماجم سنة (٨٣ هـ). انظر ترجمته في سير أعلام النبلاء ٤/٣٧١.

(٧٥) قال السيوطي في المناهل رقم (٣٥): «أبو نعيم في الدلائل، وابن مردويه في تفسيره من طريق أبي يحي التيمي، وهو وضَّاع، عن سيف بن وهب، وهو ضعيف، عن أبي الطفيل» وسيعيده المصنف برقم (٦٢١). وقال العلامة ابن

Abū ʿAbd al-Raḥmān al-Sulamī reported from Jaʿfar al-Ṣādiq that the letters "*Yā Sīn*"[145] stood for "*Yā sayyid*", meaning "O noble one", and were addressing the Prophet ﷺ. Ibn ʿAbbās said they stood for "*Yā insān*", meaning "O humankind", and again signified Muhammad ﷺ. He added: "It is an oath taken by Allah, and one of His names for the Prophet ﷺ."

Al-Zajjāj[146] said: "It was said to mean 'O Muhammad', 'O man', or 'O humankind'." Ibn al-Ḥanafiyyah[147] said: "'*Yā Sīn*'[148] means 'O Muhammad'." Kaʿb commented: "'*Yā Sīn*'[149] is an oath Allah Exalted made two thousand years before He created heaven and earth, and it means: 'O Muhammad! You are truly one of the messengers.'"

If we follow the opinion that "*Yā Sīn*" is one of the names of Muhammad ﷺ, and it is also an oath, then it strengthens and emphasizes the second oath that follows: "By the Qur'an, rich in wisdom!" If we take "*Yā Sīn*" to be Allah Exalted calling His Prophet ﷺ, then the oath that comes afterwards suffices in confirming his Prophethood. When the two oaths are taken in conjunction, Allah Exalted swears first by the name of the Prophet ﷺ and then by His Book, that Muhammad ﷺ was certainly a Messenger, delivering His Revelation to His servants, and guided to the Straight Path by his faith,

---

from the names of the Prophet ﷺ, this is not correct. This position is not supported by any *ṣaḥīḥ*, *ḥasan*, or *mursal* hadith, neither is it mentioned by any Companion. Rather, they are letters [that are found in the Qur'an], just like '*Alif Lām Mīm*', '*Ḥā Mīm*', '*Alif Lām Rā*', and other examples."

145 *Yā Sīn*, 1.

146 Ibrāhīm ibn Muhammad al-Baghdādī, a leading grammarian of his generation. He passed away in 311 AH (although there is some difference of opinion regarding this date). See *Siyar Aʿlām al-Nubalāʾ* (14/360).

147 Muhammad ibn al-Ḥanafiyyah, the son of ʿAlī ibn Abī Ṭālib. His mother, Khawlah bint Jaʿfar al-Ḥanafiyyah, was a prisoner of war from the Battle of Yamāmah. He was born in the same year that Abū Bakr passed away, and he died in 80 AH (with some difference of opinion). See *Siyar Aʿlām al-Nubalāʾ* (4/110) for a lengthy biography.

148 *Yā Sīn*, 1.

149 ibid.

وحكى أبو عبد الرحمن السُّلَمِيُّ، عن جَعْفرٍ الصادق - رَحِمَهُ اللهُ تعالى - أنه أراد: يا سيِّدُ! مخاطبةً لنبيه صلى الله عليه وسلم. وعن ابن عباس: ﴿يس﴾ يا إنْسان! أرادَ محمداً صلى الله عليه وسلم. وقال: هو قَسَمٌ، وهو من أَسْماء الله تعالى. وقال الزجّاج(٧٦): قيلَ: معناه يا محمد! وقيل: يا رَجُل! وقيل: يا إنسان!

وعن ابْنِ الحنَفِية(٧٧): ﴿يس﴾: يا محمد! وعن كَعْب: ﴿يس﴾ قَسَمٌ أَقسم اللهُ تعالى به قَبْلَ أنْ يَخلُقَ السماءَ والأرضَ بأَلْفَيْ عام: يا محمَّدُ! إنكَ لمنَ المرسلين. ثم قال: ﴿وَالْقُرْآنِ الْحَكِيمِ (٢) إِنَّكَ لَمِنَ الْمُرْسَلِينَ﴾ [يس: ٢، ٣]. فإنْ قُدِّرَ(٧٨) أنه من(٧٩) أسمائه صلى الله عليه وسلم، وصَحَّ(٨٠) فيه أنه قسَمٌ، كان فيه من التعظيم ما تقدَّمَ، ويؤكِّدُ فيه القَسَم عطفُ القَسَمِ الآخَرِ عليه، وإنْ كان بمعنى النداء فقد جاء قَسَمٌ آخر بعْدَه لتحقيقِ رِسالته، والشهادةِ بهدايته. أقسم [الله] تعالى باسْمِه وكتابهِ

قيم الجوزية في تحفة المودود ص (٩٣) بتحقيقي: «وأما ما يذكره العوام أن ﴿يس﴾ و ﴿طه﴾ من أسماء النبي صلى الله عليه وسلم فغير صحيح، ليس ذلك في حديث صحيح، ولا حسن، ولا مرسل، ولا أثر عن صاحب، وإنما هذه الحروف مثل ﴿الم﴾ و ﴿حم﴾ و ﴿الر﴾ ونحوها».

(٧٦) هو إبراهيم بن محمد البغدادي. نحوي زمانه. مات سنة (٣١١ هـ) على خلاف في ذلك. انظر ترجمته في سير أعلام النبلاء ١٤/٣٦٠.

(٧٧) هو محمد بن الإمام علي بن أبي طالب. من كبار التابعين. أمه من سبي اليمامة وهي خولة بنت جعفر الحنفية. ولد في العام الذي مات فيه أبو بكر، ومات سنة (٨٠ هـ) على خلاف في ذلك. له ترجمة مطولة في سير أعلام النبلاء ٤/١١٠.

(٧٨) في المطبوع: «قرّر». ومعنى «قُدِّرَ»: فُرِض.

(٧٩) في المطبوع: «بين».

(٨٠) في المطبوع: «وَضَحَ». ومعنى «صَحَّ»: ثبت.

a path without any crookedness or deviation from the truth. As al-Naqāsh highlighted: "In His Book, Allah Exalted did not swear by any Prophet to confirm their Prophethood except for Muhammad ﷺ." The Prophet ﷺ said: "I am the master of the children of Adam [and I am not boasting]."[150] Allah Exalted said: "I do swear by this city [of Makkah] – even though you [O Prophet] are subject to abuse in this city."[151] Makkī interpreted the verses with a different meaning, saying: "I do not swear by this city after you have been ejected from it." Another view says that the word "*Lā*" at the beginning of the surah, which Makkī understood as "Do not", actually reinforces the oath. There are also two readings of the second verse, which is either interpreted as "You [O Muhammad] are permissible in this city", or "Whatever you do [O Muhammad] in this city is permissible." It is generally accepted by scholars of *tafsīr* that the city being referred to is Makkah. Al-Wāsiṭī, on the other hand, said it was Madinah, expressing the verses as: "We swear to you by this city (i.e., Madinah) which was honoured by your presence in life and your blessings after death." The first opinion is more likely to be correct because the surah was revealed whilst the Prophet ﷺ was still in Makkah. Ibn 'Aṭā' says something similar in his commentary on the verse: "And this secure city [of Makkah]!"[152] He stated: "Allah Exalted made the city secure because of the residence of the Prophet ﷺ, who brings safety and security to wherever he is present.

Next, Allah Exalted said: "And by every parent and [their] child!"[153] Some said the verse refers to Adam, which would make it a general statement, whereas some believed it to refer to Prophet

---

150 Reported by Muslim (2278) from the hadith of Abū Hurayrah, without the phrase: "And I am not boasting".

151 *al-Balad*, 1-2.

152 *al-Tīn*, 3.

153 *al-Balad*, 3.

إنه لَمِنَ المُرْسَلِين بوَحْيه إلى عِبَادِه، وعلى صراطٍ مستقيم من إيمانِه، أي طريقٌ لا اعْوِجاجَ فيه، ولا عُدولَ عن الحق. قال النَّقاشُ(٨١) : لم يُقْسِم الله تعالى لأحدٍ من أنبيائه بالرسالة في كتاب إلَّا له، وفيه مِنْ تَعظيمه وتَمْجِيدِه - على تأويل مَنْ قال: أنه يا سيِّد! مافيه.

٢٥- وقد قال عليه السلام: «أنا سيِّدُ ولَدِ آدَمَ [ولا فخر]»(٨٢). وقال تعالى: ﴿لَا أُقْسِمُ بِهَٰذَا الْبَلَدِ (١) وَأَنتَ حِلٌّ بِهَٰذَا الْبَلَدِ﴾ [البلد: ١، ٢]. قيل: لا أُقْسِمُ به إذا لم تكُنْ فيه بعد خُروجِكَ منه، حكاه مَكِّيٌّ. وقيل: (لا) زائدة؛ أي أُقسم به وأَنْتَ به يا محمد! حَلَالٌ. أو حِلٌّ لكَ ما فَعَلت فيه على التفسيرين. والمرادُ بالبلد عند هؤلاء: مكّة. وقال الوَاسِطِيُّ: أي نَحلِف لك بهذا البلدِ الذي شَرَّفْتَه بمكانك فيه حياً، وبركتك مَيّتاً، يَعْني: المدينة. والأولُ أصحُّ؛ لأن السورة مكية، وما بعده يُصَحِّحهُ قوله تعالى: ﴿وَأَنتَ حِلٌّ بِهَٰذَا الْبَلَدِ﴾ [البلد: ٢]. ونَحْوُه قولُ ابن عطاء في تفسير قولِه تعالى: ﴿وَهَٰذَا الْبَلَدِ الْأَمِينِ﴾ [التين: ٣]. قال: آمنها الله [تعالى] بمُقامِهِ فيها وكَوْنِه بها، فإنَّ كَوْنَه أَمَانٌ حيثُ كان. ثم قال تعالى: ﴿وَوَالِدٍ وَمَا وَلَدَ﴾ [البلد: ٣] [و] من قال: أراد آدم فهو عامّ؛ ومَنْ قال: هو إبراهيم وما وَلد فهي(٨٣) - إن شاءَ اللهُ - إشارةٌ إلى محمد ﷺ،

---

(٨١) هو العلامة المفسّر، شيخ القراء محمد بن الحسن الموصلي ولد سنة (٢٦٦ هـ). ومات سنة (٣٥١ هـ). انظر ترجمته في السير ٥٧٣/١٥

(٨٢) أخرجه مسلم (٢٢٧٨) من حديث أبي هريرة بدون قوله: ولا فخر.

(٨٣) كلمة «فهي»، لم ترد في المطبوع.

Ibrāhīm and his offspring, which would point towards Muhammad ﷺ. If the latter opinion is correct, then Allah Exalted swears by the Prophet ﷺ twice within this surah.

The words of Allah Exalted at the beginning of Surah al-Baqarah, "*Alif Lām Mīm*. This is the Book! There is no doubt about it"[154], were also subject to different interpretations. Ibn 'Abbās said that the letters "*Alif Lām Mīm*"[155] are an oath, although other explanations were recorded from him and others. Sahl ibn 'Abdullāh al-Tustarī said: "The '*Alif*' stands for Allah Exalted, the '*Lām*' for Jibrīl n, and the '*Mīm*' for Muhammad ﷺ." A similar statement was reported from al-Samarqandī, but he did not attribute it to Sahl. Al-Samarqandī gave the meaning as: "Allah Exalted sent Jibrīl to Muhammad ﷺ with this Qur'an, the book with no doubt in it." Again, this reading combines oaths taken by Allah Exalted upon the Qur'an and upon Muhammad ﷺ. Ibn 'Aṭā' said that the letter "*Qāf*" in "*Qāf*. By the glorious Qur'an!"[156] stands for the "*quwwah*", or "strength", of the heart of Muhammad ﷺ which managed to bear the weight of Divine Revelation. "*Qāf*" was also said to be another name for the Qur'an, a particular mountain, or other than that. Ja'far ibn Muhammad al-Ṣādiq said that the verse "By the stars when they fade away!"[157], which he understood as "By the star", refers to Muhammad ﷺ. He said that "the star" is the heart of Muhammad ﷺ, which is filled with light and connected solely to Allah. Ibn 'Aṭā' said that "the dawn" ("*al-fajr*") in the words of Allah Exalted "By the dawn, and the ten nights,"[158] is Muhammad ﷺ, because of the light and faith that emanate (*tafajjara*) from him.

---

154 *al-Baqarah*, 1-2.

155 *al-Baqarah*, 1.

156 *Qāf*, 1.

157 *al-Najm*, 1.

158 *al-Fajr*, 1-2.

فتتضمَّنُ السورةُ القَسَم به - عليه السلام - في موضعين. وقال تعالى: ﴿الم (١) ذَٰلِكَ الْكِتَابُ لَا رَيْبَ ۛ فِيهِ﴾ [البقرة: ١، ٢]. قال ابنُ عباس: هذه الحروفُ أقسَامٌ، أقسمَ الله [تعالىٰ] بها. وعنه وعن غَيْرِه فيها غَيْرُ ذلك. وقال سَهْلُ بن عَبْد اللهِ التُّسْتَرِيُّ: الألف: هو الله تعالى. واللام: جبريل. والميم: محمد عليه السلام. وحكى هذا القولَ السَّمَرْقَنْدِيُّ، ولم ينسبه إلىٰ سَهْل، وجعل معناه: اللهُ أنزل جبريل على محمد بهذا القرآن لا رَيْبَ فيه، وعلى الوَجْه الأول يحتمل القَسَمُ أنَّ هذا الكتابَ حقٌّ لا رَيْبَ فيه، وعلى الوَجْه الأول يحتمل القَسَمُ أنَّ هذا الكتابَ حقٌّ لا رَيْبَ فيه، ثُمَّ فيه مِنْ فَضِيلته[(٨٤)] قِرَانُ اسْمِه [باسمه] نحو ما تقدم. وقال ابنُ عطاء في قوله تعالى: ﴿ق ۚ وَالْقُرْآنِ الْمَجِيدِ﴾ [ق: ١]: أقسم بقُوَّةِ قَلْب حبيبه [محمد] صلى الله عليه وسلم حيث حمل الخِطَابَ والمشاهدةَ ولم يؤثر ذلك فيه لعُلُوِّ حاله. وقيل: هو اسْمٌ للقرآن. وقيل: هو اسْمٌ للهِ [تعالى]. وقيل: جَبَلٌ مُحِيط بالأرض. وقيل غير هذا. وقال جَعْفَر بن محمد في تَفْسير: ﴿وَالنَّجْمِ إِذَا هَوَىٰ﴾ [النجم: ١]: أنه محمد صلى الله عليه وسلم، وقال: ﴿النجم﴾: قَلْبُ محمد [صلى الله عليه وسلم]، ﴿هوى﴾[(٨٥)]: انشرح من الأنوار. وقال: انقطَع عن غير الله. وقال ابنُ عَطَاء في قوله تعالى: ﴿وَالْفَجْرِ (١) وَلَيَالٍ عَشْرٍ﴾ [الفجر: ١، ٢] الفَجر: محمد [صلى الله عليه وسلم] لأنَّ منه تفَجَّر الإيمانُ (١٠/أ).

---

(٨٤) في المطبوع: «فضيلة».

(٨٥) كلمة «هوى»، لم ترد في المطبوع.

Allah Exalted Takes an Oath to Confirm the Station of the Prophet ﷺ With Him

Allah ﷻ said: "By the morning sunlight, and the night when it falls still! Your Lord [O Prophet] has not abandoned you, nor has He become hateful [of you]. And the next life is certainly far better for you than this one. And [surely] your Lord will give so much to you that you will be pleased. Did He not find you as an orphan then sheltered you? Did He not find you unguided then guided you? And did He not find you needy then satisfied your needs? So do not oppress the orphan, nor repulse the beggar. And proclaim the blessings of your Lord."[159] The scholars of *tafsīr* differed regarding the circumstances of the revelation of this surah. Some said that Jibrīl ﷺ was delayed from visiting the Prophet ﷺ with Divine Revelation, so a woman from the Quraysh began to talk about him, and then the surah was sent down.[160] Others said it was a group of idol worshippers who started rumours about the lapse in revelation.[161] In any case, the surah includes six ways in which Allah Exalted praises and honours the Prophet ﷺ:

1. Allah Exalted takes an oath to emphasize the situation the Prophet ﷺ was facing, saying: "By the morning sunlight, and the night when it falls still!"[162] The implied meaning of the oath is: "By the Lord of the morning sunlight". Taking an oath in this manner is

---

159 *al-Ḍuḥā*, 1-11.

160 Reported by Bukhārī (1125) and Muslim (1797/115) from the hadith of Jundub ibn ʿAbdullāh.

161 Reported by Tirmidhī (3345), also from the hadith of Jundub, and he said: "This narration is *ḥasan ṣaḥīḥ*." See also, Bukhārī (2802).

162 *al-Ḍuḥā*, 1-2.

الفصل الخامس

في قَسَمِهِ - تعالى جَدُّهُ - له، لِيُحقِّق مَكانَتَهُ عِنْدَهُ

قال جلَّ اسْمُه: ﴿وَالضُّحَىٰ (١) وَاللَّيْلِ إِذَا سَجَىٰ (٢) مَا وَدَّعَكَ رَبُّكَ وَمَا قَلَىٰ (٣) وَلَلْآخِرَةُ خَيْرٌ لَّكَ مِنَ الْأُولَىٰ (٤) وَلَسَوْفَ يُعْطِيكَ رَبُّكَ فَتَرْضَىٰ (٥) أَلَمْ يَجِدْكَ يَتِيمًا فَآوَىٰ (٦) وَوَجَدَكَ ضَالًّا فَهَدَىٰ (٧) وَوَجَدَكَ عَائِلًا فَأَغْنَىٰ (٨) فَأَمَّا الْيَتِيمَ فَلَا تَقْهَرْ (٩) وَأَمَّا السَّائِلَ فَلَا تَنْهَرْ (١٠) وَأَمَّا بِنِعْمَةِ رَبِّكَ فَحَدِّثْ (١١)﴾ [الضحى: ١ - ١١] اختلف في سبب نزول هذه السورة.

٢٦- فقيل: كان تَرْكُ النبيِّ ﷺ قيامَ الليل لعُذْرٍ نزل به، فتكلمتْ امرأةٌ في ذلك بكلام(٨٦).

٢٧- وقيل: بَلْ تكلَّمَ به المشركون عند فَتْرَة الوحي، فنزلت هذه(٨٧) السورة(٨٨). قال القاضي الإمام أبو الفَضل رحمه الله: تضمَّنَتْ هذه السورةُ من كرامةِ الله تعالى له، وتَنْوِيهه به، وتعظِيمه إياه ستَّةَ وجوه:

الأول: القَسَم له عما أخبره به مِنْ حاله بقوله [تعالى]: ﴿وَالضُّحَىٰ

---

(٨٦) أخرج ذلك البخاري (١١٢٥)، ومسلم (١١٥/١٧٩٧) من حديث جندب بن عبد الله.

(٨٧) كلمة: «هذه» لم ترد في المطبوع.

(٨٨) ورد هذا في حديث جندب عند الترمذي (٣٣٤٥) وقال: «حديث حسن صحيح». وانظر البخاري (٢٨٠٢).

the highest form of commendation.

2. Allah Exalted clarifies the status of the Prophet ﷺ with Him, saying: "Your Lord [O Prophet] has not abandoned you, nor has He become hateful [of you]."[163] The verses were also interpreted to mean: "He has not neglected you after choosing you."
3. In regards to the verse, "And the next life is certainly far better for you than this one"[164], Ibn Isḥāq[165] said: "Meaning: 'what is waiting for you with Allah is greater than what He has given you in this life.'" Sahl interpreted the verses as: "The intercession and noble station I have granted you in the Hereafter are better than what I have given you in this life."
4. Then, Allah Exalted says: "And [surely] your Lord will give so much to you that you will be pleased."[166] This verse links the honour and contentedness of the Prophet ﷺ with the promise of His Blessings and Abundance in this life and the Hereafter. Ibn Isḥāq said: "Allah Exalted will please the Prophet ﷺ with victory in this life and reward in the Hereafter." Others commented: "He will grant the Prophet ﷺ the Pond [of Abundance][167] and intercession [in the Hereafter]." It was related from some family members of the Prophet ﷺ that he said: "There is no verse more hopeful, and it would not please me for anyone from my nation to enter the Hellfire."[168]
5. In the next part of the surah, Allah Exalted enumerates His Bless-

---

163 *al-Ḍuḥā*, 3.

164 *al-Ḍuḥā*, 4.

165 Muhammad ibn Isḥāq, a leading authority on historical battles and biographies (including his famous biography of the Prophet ﷺ). He passed away in 150 AH (although some say he died later than that). See *Siyar A'lām al-Nubalā'* (7/33).

166 *al-Ḍuḥā*, 5.

167 Al-Ḥawḍ [al-Kawthar].

168 Reported by Abū Nu'aym in *Al-Ḥilyah*, in a *mawqūf* narration from 'Alī, and by Daylamī, in *Musnad al-Firdaws*, in a *marfū* narration. See also, *Al-Manāhil*, p. 43.

(١) وَاللَّيْلِ إِذَا سَجَىٰ﴾. أي ورَبِّ الضحى، وهذا مِنْ أعظمِ درجات المَبَرَّة[٨٩].

الثاني: بَيَانُ مكانتِه عنده وحُظْوَته لدَيْهِ بقوله تعالى: ﴿مَا وَدَّعَكَ رَبُّكَ وَمَا قَلَىٰ﴾؛ أي: ماتركَكَ وما أَبْغَضك. وقيل: ما أَهْمَلَك بعد أن اصْطَفاك.

الثالث: قوله تعالى: ﴿وَلَلْآخِرَةُ خَيْرٌ لَّكَ مِنَ الْأُولَىٰ﴾؛ قال ابن إسحاق[٩٠]: أي مَآلكَ في مَرْجِعِكَ عند الله أَعظَمُ ممّا أعطاكَ من كرامةِ الدُّنيا. وقال سَهْلٌ: أي ما ادَّخَرْتُ[٩١] لك من الشفاعة والمَقَام المحمود خَيْرٌ لكَ مما أعطيتُكَ في الدنيا.

الرابع: قوله [تعالى]: ﴿وَلَسَوْفَ يُعْطِيكَ رَبُّكَ فَتَرْضَىٰ﴾. وهذه آيةٌ جامعةٌ لوجوهِ الكرامة، وأنواعِ السعادة، وشَتَاتِ الإنْعَام في الدَّارَين، والزيادةِ. قال ابن إسحاق: يُرضِيه بالفُلْج[٩٢] في الدنيا، والثوابِ في الآخرة. وقيل: يُعْطيه الحَوْضَ والشفاعة.

٢٨- ورُوي عن بعض آل النبي ﷺ أنه قال: ليس آيةٌ في القرآن أَرْجَى

---

(٨٩) على هامش الأصل زيادة: «للنبوة» وفوقها علامة الصحة.

(٩٠) هو محمد بن إسحاق إمام أهل المغازي والسير. مات سنة (١٥٠ هـ) ويقال بعدها. انظر ترجمته في سير أعلام النبلاء ٧/٣٣.

(٩١) في المطبوع: «ما ذخرت» من الذخيرة، وهي الشيء النفيس يخبأ.

(٩٢) الفُلْجُ بالضم الاسمُ. وبالفتح المصدر، وهو الفوز والظفر. انتهى من هامش الأصل.

ings upon the Prophet ﷺ. He guided him (or guided people by him, depending on the interpretation of the verse), He enriched him after poverty (with material wealth or with the contentment He placed in his heart, again depending on the interpretation), and He found him as an orphan and sent his uncle to care for him and provide him with shelter. An alternative understanding of the verse says that he found shelter with Allah Exalted. Others said that the description of the Prophet ﷺ as "an orphan" signifies that there was no one like him and that he was sheltered by Allah Exalted. Others gave the meaning of the verses as: "Did We not find you and then guide the misguided, enrich the poor, and provide shelter for orphans through you [O Prophet]?" The verses are a reminder of all His Blessings, as if to say: "If Allah Exalted did not abandon, neglect, or become angry with the Prophet ﷺ when he was young, poor, an orphan, and unknown, then how could He after choosing him and raising his status?"

6. Finally, Allah Exalted commands the Prophet ﷺ to openly declare His Blessings upon him: "And proclaim the blessings of your Lord."[169] Undoubtedly, the one who is grateful for blessings displays their gratitude, and this instruction applies both specifically to the Prophet ﷺ and generally to all Muslims.

Allah Exalted said: "By the stars when they fade away! Your fellow man is neither misguided nor astray. Nor does he speak of his own whims. It is only a Revelation sent down [to him]. He has been taught by one [Angel] of mighty power and great perfection, who once rose to [his] true form, while on the highest point above the horizon, then he approached [the Prophet ﷺ], coming so close that he was only two arms-lengths away or even less. Then Allah revealed to His servant what He revealed [through Gabriel]. The heart [of the

---

169 *al-Ḍuḥā*, 11.

منها، ولا يَرْضَى رسولُ الله ﷺ أَنْ يَدْخُلَ أحدٌ من أُمته النارَ(٩٣).

الخامس: ما عدَّهُ(٩٤) تعالى عليه من نِعَمِهِ، وقرَّره من آلائه قِبَلَه في بقية السورة؛ من هدايته إلى ما هدَاه له، أو هدايَةِ الناس به على اختلاف التفاسير، ولا مالَ له ؛ فأغناه اللهُ(٩٥) بما آتاه، أو بما جعَلَه في قَلْبِه من القناعة والغنى، ويتيماً فَحَدِبَ عليه(٩٦) عمُّه، وآواه إليه. وقيل :آواه إلى الله. وقيل: يتيماً: لا مِثَالَ(٩٧) لك (١٠/ب) فآواك إليه. وقيل: المعنى: ألم يجدكَ فهَدَى بكَ ضالًّا، وأَغنى بكَ عائلاً، وآوي بك يتيماً، ذَكَّرَهُ بهذه المِنِن، وأنه - على المعلوم من التفسير - لم يُهمِلْه في حال صغره، وعَيْلَتِه(٩٨)،ويُتْمه، وقَبْلَ معرفته به، ولا ودَّعه(٩٩)، ولا قَلَاه(١٠٠)، فكيف بعد اختصاصه واصطفائه!

السادس: أَمْرُه بإظهار نعمته عليه، وشُكْرِه ما شرَّفَه به(١٠١)، بنَشْرِهِ،

---

(٩٣) أخرجه أبو نعيم في «الحلية» عن علي موقوفاً، وأخرجه الديلمي في مسند الفردوس من حديثه مرفوعاً/ المناهل رقم (٤٣).

(٩٤) (عدَّه): ذكره. وفي المطبوع عَدده

(٩٥) لفظ الجلالة: «الله»، لم يرد في المطبوع.

(٩٦) حدب عليه: عطف عليه، ورقَّ له.

(٩٧) في نسخة: (لا مالَ).

(٩٨) وعَيْلته: وفقره.

(٩٩) ولا ودعه: أي ما تركه منذ اختاره.

(١٠٠) ولا قلاه: أي ما أبغضه منذ أحبه.

(١٠١) كلمة: «به»، لم ترد في المطبوع.

Prophet ﷺ] did not doubt what he saw. How can you [O pagans] then dispute with him regarding what he saw? And he certainly saw that [Angel descend] a second time at the Lote Tree of the most extreme limit [in the seventh heaven] – near which is the Garden of [Eternal] Residence – while the Lote Tree was overwhelmed with [heavenly] splendours! The sight [of the Prophet ﷺ] never wandered, nor did it overreach. He certainly saw some of his Lord's greatest signs."[170]

The scholars differed about the meaning of "the star" ("*al-najm*") in the first verse of the surah. Interpretations of "*al-najm*" include its apparent meaning (i.e., "a star") and "the Qur'an". Ja'far ibn Muhammad al-Ṣādiq said: "It refers to the heart of Muhammad ﷺ." Similarly, al-Sulamī considered "the star" in Surah al-Ṭāriq to refer to the Prophet ﷺ, in the words of Allah Exalted: "By the heaven and the nightly star! And what will make you realize what the nightly star is? [It is] the star of piercing brightness."[171]

The verses in Surah al-Najm affirm the abundant virtues of the Prophet ﷺ. Allah b swears upon the guidance and truthfulness of the Prophet ﷺ, and that he does not speak "of his own whims"[172]. He affirms that the Prophet ﷺ received Divine Revelation from Him, delivered by Jibrīl n, an "[Angel] of mighty power"[173]. Next, Allah Exalted informs us of the miraculous Night Journey, which ended "...at the Lote Tree of the most extreme limit [in the seventh heaven]". He confirms the veracity of what the Prophet ﷺ saw on that journey, including "some of his Lord's greatest signs"[174]. These signs are also mentioned at the beginning of Surah al-Isrā': "...so that We

---

170 *al-Najm*, 1-18.

171 *al-Ṭāriq*, 1-3.

172 *al-Najm*, 3.

173 *al-Najm*, 5.

174 *al-Najm*, 18.

وإشادةِ ذِكْره بقوله [تعالى]: ﴿وَأَمَّا بِنِعْمَةِ رَبِّكَ فَحَدِّثْ﴾ [الضحى: ١١]؛ فإن مِنْ شُكْرِ النعمة الحديث بها؛ وهذا خاصٌّ له، عامٌّ لأمته.

وقال تعالى: ﴿وَالنَّجْمِ إِذَا هَوَىٰ (١) مَا ضَلَّ صَاحِبُكُمْ وَمَا غَوَىٰ (٢) وَمَا يَنطِقُ عَنِ الْهَوَىٰ (٣) إِنْ هُوَ إِلَّا وَحْيٌ يُوحَىٰ (٤) عَلَّمَهُ شَدِيدُ الْقُوَىٰ (٥) ذُو مِرَّةٍ فَاسْتَوَىٰ (٦) وَهُوَ بِالْأُفُقِ الْأَعْلَىٰ (٧) ثُمَّ دَنَا فَتَدَلَّىٰ (٨) فَكَانَ قَابَ قَوْسَيْنِ أَوْ أَدْنَىٰ (٩) فَأَوْحَىٰ إِلَىٰ عَبْدِهِ مَا أَوْحَىٰ (١٠) مَا كَذَبَ الْفُؤَادُ مَا رَأَىٰ (١١) أَفَتُمَارُونَهُ عَلَىٰ مَا يَرَىٰ (١٢) وَلَقَدْ رَآهُ نَزْلَةً أُخْرَىٰ (١٣) عِندَ سِدْرَةِ الْمُنتَهَىٰ (١٤) عِندَهَا جَنَّةُ الْمَأْوَىٰ (١٥) إِذْ يَغْشَى السِّدْرَةَ مَا يَغْشَىٰ (١٦) مَا زَاغَ الْبَصَرُ وَمَا طَغَىٰ (١٧) لَقَدْ رَأَىٰ مِنْ آيَاتِ رَبِّهِ الْكُبْرَىٰ (١٨)﴾ [النجم: ١ - ١٨]. اختلف المفسرون في قوله [تعالى]: ﴿وَالنَّجْمِ﴾ بأقاوِيلَ معروفة، منها النَّجم على ظاهره، ومنها القرآن. وعن جعفر بن محمد؛ أنه محمدٌ عليه السلام؛ وقال: هو قَلْبُ محمدٍ.

وقد قيل في قوله [تعالى]: ﴿وَالسَّمَاءِ وَالطَّارِقِ (١) وَمَا أَدْرَاكَ مَا الطَّارِقُ (٢) النَّجْمُ الثَّاقِبُ (٣)﴾ [الطارق: ١ - ٣] إن النجم هنا أيضاً محمد ﷺ؛ حكاه السُّلَمِيّ. تضمَّنت هذه الآياتُ من فَضْله وشرفِهِ العِدِّ[١٠٢] ما يقف دونه العَدُّ، وأقسم جلَّ اسمهُ على هدايةِ المصطفى، وتَنْزِيهه عن الهوى، وصِدْقِهِ فيما تلَا، وأنَّه وَحْي يُوحى أَوْصَلَه إليه - عن

---

(١٠٢) العِدّ: الكثرة في الشيء. يقال ماءٌ عِدٌّ: أي دائم لا انقطاع لمادته. وجمعه أعداد.

may show him some of Our signs"[175]. Any other person's intellect would not bear the weight of the miraculous signs the Prophet ﷺ witnessed on that journey. So, Allah Exalted only alludes to what he saw, saying: "Then Allah revealed to His servant what He revealed [through Jibrīl]."[176] According to linguistic scholars, this rhetorical tool of allusion heightens the magnitude of the event.

Allah Exalted said: "He certainly saw some of his Lord's greatest signs."[177] A person's mind is incapable of comprehending the precise nature of the "greatest signs"[178] that are mentioned; instead, we can only wonder. Allah Exalted emphasizes that the Prophet ﷺ was protected from any harm during the miraculous journey, and confirms the purity of his limbs. This includes the purity of his heart ("The heart [of the Prophet ﷺ] did not doubt what he saw"[179]); the honesty of his tongue ("Nor does he speak of his own whims"[180]); and the accuracy of his sight ("The [Prophet's] sight never wandered, nor did it overreach."[181])

Allah Exalted says: "I do swear by the receding stars which travel and hide, and the night as it falls, and the day as it breaks! Indeed, this [Qur'an] is the Word of [Allah delivered by Jibrīl,] a noble Messenger-Angel, full of power, held in honour by the Lord of the Throne, obeyed there [in heaven], and trustworthy. And your fellow man is not insane. And he did see that [Angel] on the clear horizon, and he does not withhold [what is revealed to him of] the Unseen.

---

175 *al-Isrā'*, 1.

176 *al-Najm*, 10.

177 *al-Najm*, 18.

178 ibid.

179 *al-Najm*, 11.

180 *al-Najm*, 3.

181 *al-Najm*, 17.

الله - جبريل عليه السلام وهو الشديد القُوى. ثم أَخبر تعالى عن فضيلته بقصة الإسراءِ، وانتهائه إلى سِدْرَةِ المُنتَهى، وتصديق بَصَرِهِ فيما رأى، وأنه رأى من آيات رَبِّه الكبرى. وقد نَبَّه على مثل هذا تعالى في أول سورة الإسراء. ولما كان ما كاشفَهُ[١٠٣] - عليه السلام - من ذلك الجَبَرُوتِ، وشاهَدَهُ من عجائب المَلَكُوت لا تُحِيطُ به العبارات، ولا تستقِلُّ بحَمْل سَماع أدناه العقولُ، رمَزَ عنه تعالى بالإيماء[١٠٤] و الكناية الدالَّة على التعظيم؛ فقال [تعالى]: ﴿فَأَوْحَىٰ إِلَىٰ عَبْدِهِ مَا أَوْحَىٰ﴾.

وهذا النوعُ من الكلام يُسمِّيه أهلُ النقد والبلاغة بالوَحْي والإشارة، وهو عندهم أبْلَغُ أبوابِ الإيجاز. وقال تعالى: ﴿لَقَدْ رَأَىٰ مِنْ آيَاتِ رَبِّهِ الْكُبْرَىٰ﴾ انحسرت الأفهامُ عن تفصيل ما أَوحىٰ، وتاهَت الأحلامُ (١١/أ) في تعيين تلكَ الآياتِ الكبرى.

قال القاضي الإمام أبو الفضل رحمه الله: اشتملت هذه الآياتُ على إعلام اللهِ تعالى بِتَزْكِيَةِ جُمْلته عليه السلام، وعِصْمَتِها من الآفاتِ في هذا المَسْرَى، فزَكَّى فؤادَه ولسانَه وجَوارِحَه: فزكّى قَلْبه[١٠٥] بقوله: ﴿مَا كَذَبَ الْفُؤَادُ مَا رَأَىٰ﴾. ولسانه بقوله: ﴿وَمَا يَنطِقُ عَنِ الْهَوَىٰ﴾. وبَصَره بقوله: ﴿مَا زَاغَ الْبَصَرُ وَمَا طَغَىٰ﴾. وقال تعالى: ﴿فَلَا أُقْسِمُ بِالْخُنَّسِ

---

(١٠٣) في المطبوع زيادة: «به».

(١٠٤) في المطبوع: «بالإيماءة».

(١٠٥) في الأصل: «وقلبه»، والمثبت من المطبوع.

And this [Qur'an] is not the word of an outcast devil."[182]

Allah Exalted takes an oath to affirm that His Book was delivered by "a noble Messenger-Angel"[183]; meaning, noble and honoured with the One who sent him. The angel, Jibrīl, was "full of power"[184] and able to convey the Divine Revelation he was entrusted with, and "held in honour"[185], firm in his status with his Lord. Jibrīl is "obeyed there"[186] (i.e., in the heavens) and "trustworthy"[187] in delivering Revelation. Although ʿAlī ibn ʿĪsā and a group of scholars took the opinion that "a noble Messenger"[188] actually refers to Muhammad ﷺ and therefore all the characteristics that follow apply to him, most understood the verses to refer to Jibrīl ﷺ. The verse "And he did see…"[189] indicates something that Muhammad ﷺ witnessed. Some commentators suggest that he saw his Lord, whilst others say it was Jibrīl ﷺ in his true form.

Allah Exalted says: "and he does not withhold [what is revealed to him of] the Unseen."[190] The word "*biḍanīn*", translated here as "he does not withhold", is found in some recitations with the letter *ẓa*, as "*biẓanīn*"[191]. According to this reading, the meaning of the verse is that the Prophet ﷺ has no apprehension or doubt about the Unseen. According to those who recite "*biḍanīn*", the meaning is that the Prophet ﷺ is never stingy in reminding people of the Unseen

---

182 *al-Takwīr*, 15-25.

183 *al-Takwīr*, 19.

184 *al-Takwīr*, 20.

185 ibid.

186 *al-Takwīr*, 21.

187 ibid.

188 *al-Takwīr*, 19.

189 *al-Takwīr*, 23.

190 *al-Takwīr*, 24.

191 This was the recitation of Ibn Kathīr, Abū ʿAmr, al-Kisāʾī, and Yaʿqūb. See *Al-Mabsūṭ fī al-Qirāʾāt al-*ʿAshar, by Ibn Mihrān (p. 464).

(١٥) الْجَوَارِ الْكُنَّسِ[١٠٦] (١٦) وَاللَّيْلِ إِذَا عَسْعَسَ (١٧) وَالصُّبْحِ إِذَا تَنَفَّسَ (١٨) إِنَّهُ لَقَوْلُ رَسُولٍ كَرِيمٍ (١٩) ذِى قُوَّةٍ عِندَ ذِى الْعَرْشِ مَكِينٍ (٢٠) مُّطَاعٍ ثَمَّ أَمِينٍ (٢١) وَمَا صَاحِبُكُم بِمَجْنُونٍ (٢٢) وَلَقَدْ رَآهُ بِالْأُفُقِ الْمُبِينِ (٢٣) وَمَا هُوَ عَلَى الْغَيْبِ بِضَنِينٍ (٢٤) وَمَا هُوَ بِقَوْلِ شَيْطَانٍ رَّجِيمٍ (٢٥)﴾[التكوير: ١٥-٢٥]. ﴿لا أقسم﴾: أي أُقسم. ﴿إنه لقول رسُولٍ كَريم﴾: أي كريم عند مرسله. ﴿ذى قُوَّةٍ﴾: على تبليغ ما حمله من الوَحْي، ﴿مكين﴾: أي متمكِّنُ المنزلة من ربِّه، رَفِيع المَحَلِّ عنده، ﴿مُطَاع ثَمَّ﴾: أي في السماء. ﴿أمين﴾: على الوَحْي. قال علي بن عيسى[١٠٧] وغيره: الرسولُ الكريمُ - هنا محمدٌ ﷺ. فجميعُ الأوصافِ بَعْدُ على هذا له. وقال غيره: هو جبريل عليه السلام، فترجع الأوصافُ إليه.

﴿ولقد رآه﴾: يعني محمّداً. قيل: رأى ربَّه. وقيل رأَى جبريلَ في صورته.

﴿وما هو على الغيب بظنين﴾[١٠٨]، أي: بِمُتَّهَمٍ. ومن قرأَهُ[١٠٩] بالضاد فمعناه: ماهو ببخيل بالدعاء به، والتذكير بحكمِه وبعلمه، وهذه لمحمد عليه

---

(١٠٦) بالخنّس الجوار الكُنَّس: بالكواكب السيارة، تخنُس نهاراً، وتختفي عن البصر، وهي فوق الأفق، وتظهر ليلاً ثم تكنِسُ وتستتر في مغيبها تحت الأفق (كلمات القرآن لمخلوف).

(١٠٧) علامة نحوي معتزلي، صنف في التفسير واللغة والنحو والكلام. مات سنة (٣٨٤ هـ) عن (٨٨) سنة. انظر ترجمته في سير أعلام النبلاء ١٦/٥٣٣.

(١٠٨) وهي قراءة ابن كثير وأبي عمْرِو، والكسائي، ويعقوب. وقرأ الباقون: (بضنين): بالضاد (المبسوط في القراءات العشر لابن مِهران ص: ٤٦٤).

(١٠٩) (قرأه) أي هذا اللفظ. وفي المطبوع: «قرأها»: أي هذه الآية أو الكلمة.

and conveying his knowledge about it. By consensus of opinion, this section of the surah refers to Muhammad ﷺ.

Allah Exalted says: "Nūn. By the pen and what everyone writes! By the grace of your Lord, you [O Prophet] are not insane. You will certainly have a never-ending reward. And you are truly [a man] of outstanding character. Soon you and the pagans will see, which of you is mad. Surely your Lord [alone] knows best who has strayed from His Way and who is [rightly] guided. So do not give in to the deniers. They wish you would compromise so they would yield [to you]. And do not obey the despicable, vain oath-taker, slanderer, gossip-monger, withholder of good, transgressor, evildoer, brute, and – on top of all that – an illegitimate child. Now, [simply] because he has been blessed with [abundant] wealth and children, whenever Our Revelations are recited to him, he says, 'Ancient fables!' We will soon mark his snout."[192]

In these verses, Allah Exalted swears that His Chosen Prophet ﷺ is free from the disbelievers' accusations about him. He gently reassures him: "By the grace of your Lord, you [O Prophet] are not insane."[193] Then, Allah Exalted informs the Prophet ﷺ of the eternal, immeasurable reward awaiting him with his Lord: "You will certainly have a never-ending reward."[194] Next, He praises the Prophet ﷺ for the characteristics and guidance He blessed him with: "And you are truly [a man] of outstanding character."[195] The verse includes two particles of emphasis, "*innaka*" and "*la-*" (translated here as: "you are truly") to accentuate His honouring of the Prophet ﷺ. The "outstanding character"[196] referred to has been variously interpreted as

192 *al-Qalam*, 1-16.

193 *al-Qalam*, 2.

194 *al-Qalam*, 3.

195 *al-Qalam*, 4.

196 ibid.

السلام باتفاق. وقال تعالى: ﴿نٓ ۚ وَالْقَلَمِ وَمَا يَسْطُرُونَ (١) مَا أَنتَ بِنِعْمَةِ رَبِّكَ بِمَجْنُونٍ (٢) وَإِنَّ لَكَ لَأَجْرًا غَيْرَ مَمْنُونٍ (٣) وَإِنَّكَ لَعَلَىٰ خُلُقٍ عَظِيمٍ (٤) فَسَتُبْصِرُ وَيُبْصِرُونَ (٥) بِأَييِّكُمُ الْمَفْتُونُ (٦) إِنَّ رَبَّكَ هُوَ أَعْلَمُ بِمَن ضَلَّ عَن سَبِيلِهِ وَهُوَ أَعْلَمُ بِالْمُهْتَدِينَ (٧) فَلَا تُطِعِ الْمُكَذِّبِينَ (٨) وَدُّوا لَوْ تُدْهِنُ فَيُدْهِنُونَ (٩) وَلَا تُطِعْ كُلَّ حَلَّافٍ مَّهِينٍ (١٠) هَمَّازٍ مَّشَّاءٍ بِنَمِيمٍ (١١) مَّنَّاعٍ لِّلْخَيْرِ مُعْتَدٍ أَثِيمٍ (١٢) عُتُلٍّ بَعْدَ ذَٰلِكَ زَنِيمٍ (١٣) أَن كَانَ ذَا مَالٍ وَبَنِينَ (١٤) إِذَا تُتْلَىٰ عَلَيْهِ آيَاتُنَا قَالَ أَسَاطِيرُ الْأَوَّلِينَ (١٥) سَنَسِمُهُ عَلَى الْخُرْطُومِ﴾ [القلم: ١ - ١٦]. أقسم اللهُ تعالى بما أقسم به مِنْ عظيم قَسَمِه على تنزيه المصطفى مِمَّا غَمَصَتْه[١١٠] الكفَرةُ به،وتكذيبهم له، وآنسه، وبسط أَمَلَهُ بقوله - محسناً خطابَه - : ﴿مَا أَنتَ بِنِعْمَةِ رَبِّكَ بِمَجْنُونٍ﴾ [القلم: ٢]. و هذه نهايةُ المَبَرَّةِ في المخاطبة، وأعلى درجاتِ الآدابِ في المُحَاورة؛ ثم أَعْلَمَهُ بِمَا لَهُ عنده مِن نعيم دائم، وثَوَاب غَيْرِ منقطع، لا يأخذه عَدٌّ، ولا يُمْتَنُّ به عليه؛ فقال [تعالى]: ﴿وَإِنَّ لَكَ لَأَجْرًا غَيْرَ مَمْنُونٍ﴾ [القلم: ٣]. ثم أَثنى عليه بما منحه من هِبَاته، وهدَاهُ إليه، وأَكَّد ذلك تتميماً للتمجيد، بحَرْفَي التأكيد؛ فقال [تعالى]: ﴿وَإِنَّكَ لَعَلَىٰ خُلُقٍ عَظِيمٍ﴾ [القلم: ٤]. قيل: القرآن. وقيل الإسلام. وقيل الطَّبْعُ الكريم. وقيل ليس لك هِمَّة إلا اللهُ. قال الواسطي: أَثْنَى عليه بِحُسْنِ قَبوله لما أَسْدَاهُ إليه من نِعمه، وفضَّلَه بذلك

---

(١١٠) غَمَصَتْهُ: عاتَبَتْهُ.

"the Qur'an", "Islam", "a noble personality", or "striving with vigour solely with the purpose of achieving closeness to Allah".

Al-Wāsiṭī said: "Allah praised him for his willing acceptance of the favours bestowed upon him and that he was elevated above the rest of Creation on account of his character." Glory to Allah, the Subtle, the Generous, the Beneficent, the Praiseworthy, the One who made good deeds easy, guided people to perform them, and then praised and rewarded those who did. Glory to Allah, how vast and abundant are His Blessings!"

In the next part of the surah, Allah Exalted further consoles the Prophet ﷺ by promising a punishment for those who slandered him, and warning them: "Soon you and the pagans will see, which of you is mad. Surely your Lord [alone] knows best who has strayed from His Way and who is [rightly] guided."[197] Allah Exalted contrasts His Praise for the Prophet ﷺ with a resounding condemnation of his enemies, specifically mentioning ten of their worst characteristics: "So do not give in to the deniers. They wish you would compromise so they would yield [to you]. And do not obey the despicable, vain oath-taker, slanderer, gossip-monger, withholder of good, transgressor, evildoer, brute, and – on top of all that – an illegitimate child. Now, [simply] because he has been blessed with [abundant] wealth and children, whenever Our Revelations are recited to him, he says, 'Ancient fables!'"[198] Allah Exalted concludes the passage with a promise to complete their humiliation: "We will soon mark his snout."[199]

In this way, the Help of Allah for the Prophet ﷺ was greater than any he could provide for himself, and His rebuttal of his enemies more devastating.

---

197 *al-Qalam*, 5-7.

198 *al-Qalam*, 8-15.

199 *al-Qalam*, 16.

على غيره؛ لأنه جَبَلَهُ على ذلك الخُلق (١١/ب) فسبحان اللطيف الكريم، المحسنِ الجواد الحميد، الذي يَسَّر للخير وهدَى إليه، ثم أثنى على فاعله؛ وجازاه عليه؛ سُبْحانه، ما أغْمَر نَوَاله[١١١]! وأَوْسعَ إِفْضَاله! ثم سلَّاه عن قولهم بعد هذا بما وَعده به من عِقابهم[١١٢]، وتوعَّدهم بقوله ﴿فَسَتُبْصِرُ وَيُبْصِرُونَ (٥) بِأَييِّكُمُ الْمَفْتُونُ (٦) إِنَّ رَبَّكَ هُوَ أَعْلَمُ بِمَن ضَلَّ عَن سَبِيلِهِ وَهُوَ أَعْلَمُ بِالْمُهْتَدِينَ (٧)﴾ [القلم: ٥ - ٧]. ثم عطف بعد مَدْحِه على ذَمِّ عَدُوّه، وذِكْر سوء خُلقه، وعَدِّ معايبه، متولّياً ذلك بفَضْله، ومُنْتَصراً لنبيه؛ فذكر بضْعَ عَشْرَةَ خَصْلةً مِنْ خِصَالِ الذَّمِّ فيه بقوله: ﴿فَلَا تُطِعِ الْمُكَذِّبِينَ (٨) وَدُّوا لَوْ تُدْهِنُ فَيُدْهِنُونَ (٩) وَلَا تُطِعْ كُلَّ حَلَّافٍ مَّهِينٍ (١٠) هَمَّازٍ مَّشَّاءٍ بِنَمِيمٍ (١١) مَّنَّاعٍ لِّلْخَيْرِ مُعْتَدٍ أَثِيمٍ (١٢) عُتُلٍّ بَعْدَ ذَٰلِكَ زَنِيمٍ (١٣) أَن كَانَ ذَا مَالٍ وَبَنِينَ (١٤) إِذَا تُتْلَىٰ عَلَيْهِ آيَاتُنَا قَالَ أَسَاطِيرُ الْأَوَّلِينَ (١٥)﴾ [القلم: ٨ - ١٥]. ثم ختم ذلك بالوعيد الصادقِ لتمام[١١٣] شقائه، وخاتمةِ بَواره[١١٤] بقوله: ﴿سَنَسِمُهُ عَلَى الْخُرْطُومِ﴾ [القلم: ١٦]. فكانت نُصْرةُ اللهِ له أَتمَّ من نصرته لنفسه، وردُّه تعالىٰ علىٰ عدوه أبلغَ من ردِّه، وأثبت في دِيوان مجْدِه.

---

(١١١) ما أغمر نواله: ما أعمَّ عطاءه.

(١١٢) في الأصل: «عقباهم»، ثم ضرب عليها الناسخ وأثبت فوقها «عقابهم» وعليها علامة الصحة.

(١١٣) في نسخة: «بتمام».

(١١٤) بواره: هلاكه ودثاره.

Allah Exalted Addressing the Prophet ﷺ With Affection & Generosity

Allah Exalted said: "*Ṭā Hā*. We have not revealed the Qur'an to you [O Prophet] to cause you distress."[200] "*Ṭā Hā*"[201] was said to be one of the names of the Prophet ﷺ. Others gave the meaning of the verse as "O man" or "O human being", whilst others said they are simply separate letters with a meaning of their own. Al-Wāsiṭī said: "The letters stand for 'O pure one (*Ṭāhir*), O guider to the truth (*Hādī*)!'" Another interpretation says that the "*Ṭā*" stands for the imperative of the verb "*waṭa'a*", meaning "to tread", whilst the "*Hā*" refers to the earth; i.e., "stand on the ground with both feet, and do not tire yourself by standing on one foot". They connect this to the meaning of the verse that follows, which refers to the Prophet ﷺ tiring himself by standing in prayer for long portions of the night: "We have not revealed the Qur'an to you [O Prophet] to cause you distress."[202] Abū 'Abdullāh Muhammad ibn 'Abd al-Raḥmān and others narrated, with the permission of Abū al-Walīd al-Bājī (from whom they quoted the hadith): "Abū Dharr narrated, from Abū Muhammad al-Ḥamawī[203], from Ibrāhīm ibn Khuzaym al-Shāshī, from 'Abd ibn Ḥumayd, from Hāshim ibn al-Qāsim, from Abū Ja'far, from al-Rabī' ibn Anas, who said: 'The Prophet ﷺ used to stand on one foot and

---

200 *Ṭā Hā*, 1-2.

201 *Ṭā Hā*, 1.

202 *Ṭā Hā*, 2.

203 Translator's note: This likely refers to:

أبوعبد الله بن أحمد بن حموية محمد الحموي السرخسي

Who was the teacher of the narrator mentioned in the chain:

الحافظ أبو ذرعبد بن أحمد الهروي

الفصل السادس

فِيْ ما وَرَدَ مِنْ قَوْلِهِ تعالى فِيْ جهتِهِ عَلَيْهِ السَّلامُ مَوْرِدَ الشَّفَقَةِ والإِكرَامِ

قال تعالى: ﴿طه (١) مَا أَنزَلْنَا عَلَيْكَ الْقُرْآنَ لِتَشْقَى﴾ [طه: ١، ٢].

قيل: ﴿طه﴾: اسم من أسمائه عليه السلام، وقيل: هو اسمٌ لله، وقيل: معناه يا رَجُل! وقيل يا إنسان! وقيل: هي حروفٌ مُقَطَّعَةٌ لِمَعَانٍ.

وقال الواسطيُّ: أراد: يا طاهر! ياهادي! وقيل هو أمرٌ من الوطء. والهاءُ كناية عن الأرض. أي: اعتمد على الأرض بقدميك، ولا تُتْعِبْ نَفْسك بالاعتماد على قدم واحدة(١١٥)، وهو قولهُ تعالى: ﴿مَا أَنزَلْنَا عَلَيْكَ الْقُرْآنَ لِتَشْقَى﴾.

نزلت الآية فيما كان النَّبيُّ صلى الله عليه وسلم يتكلَّفُه من السَّهَر والتعب وقيام الليل.

٢٩- أخبرنا القاضي أبو عبد الله: محمد بن عبد الرحمن، وغَيْرُ واحد، عن القاضي أبي الوليد الباجي إجازة، ومن أَصْله نقلتُ؛ قال: حدثنا أبو ذَرّ الحافظ، قال: حدثنا أبو محمد الحَمُّوِيُّ، حدثنا إبراهيم بن خُزَيم الشَاشي قال: حدثنا عَبْدُ بن حُمَيد، حدثنا هاشم بن القاسم، عن أبي جعفر، عن

---

(١١٥) على هامش الأصل: «وهو قول أكثر المفسرين».

raise the other whilst he was praying, so Allah Exalted revealed "*Ṭā Hā*"[204], meaning, "O Muhammad, stand on the ground!", "We have not revealed the Qur'an to you [O Prophet] to cause you distress, but as a reminder to those in awe [of Allah]. [It is] a Revelation from the One Who created the earth and the high heavens."[205]"[206] Whether we understand "*Ṭā Hā*"[207] as one of the names of the Prophet ﷺ or as an oath taken by Allah, it is certainly a demonstration of His addressing him with affection and generosity. Another example of this comes in Surah al-Kahf: "Now, perhaps you [O Prophet] will grieve yourself to death over their denial, if they [continue to] disbelieve in this message."[208] The phrase to "grieve yourself to death"[209] was interpreted as: "Killing yourself with anger", "with rage", or "with anxiety".

In another address, Allah Exalted says: "Perhaps you [O Prophet] will grieve yourself to death over their disbelief."[210] Followed by: "If We willed, We could send down upon them a [compelling] sign from the heavens, leaving their necks bent in [utter] submission to it."[211] Allah says: "So proclaim what you have been commanded, and turn away from the polytheists. Surely We will be sufficient for you against the mockers, who set up [other] gods with Allah. They will soon come to know. We certainly know that your heart is truly distressed by what they say."[212] And: "[Other] messengers had already

---

204 *Ṭā Hā*, 1.

205 *Ṭā Hā*, 2-4.

206 Reported here from the chain of 'Abdullāh ibn Ḥumayd in his *Tafsīr* in a *mursal* narration. Suyūṭī said in *Al-Manāhil*, p. 44: "It was reported by Ibn Mardawayh in a *mawṣūl* narration from 'Alī…and he reported similar from Ibn 'Abbās."

207 *Ṭā Hā*, 1.

208 *al-Kahf*, 6.

209 ibid.

210 *al-Shu'arā'*, 3.

211 *al-Shu'arā'*, 4.

212 *al-Ḥijr*, 94-97.

الرَّبيع بن أنس؛ قال: كان النبيُّ ﷺ إذا صلَّى قام على رِجْل واحدة(١١٦) ورفع الأخرى؛ فأنزل الله تعالى: ﴿طه﴾ يعني: طَأَ الأرضَ، يا محمد! ﴿مَا أَنزَلْنَا عَلَيْكَ الْقُرْآنَ لِتَشْقَىٰ (٢) إِلَّا تَذْكِرَةً لِّمَن يَخْشَىٰ (٣) تَنزِيلاً مِّمَّنْ خَلَقَ الأَرْضَ وَالسَّمَوَاتِ الْعُلَى﴾(١١٧) [طه: ٢ - ٤]. ولا خفاءَ بما في هذا كلِّه من الإكرام وحُسْنِ المعاملة. وإن جعلنا ﴿طه﴾ من أسمائه عليه السلام كما قِيل، أو جُعِلت قَسَماً لَحِق الفَصْلُ بما قبله. ومثلُ هذا من نَمَطِ(١١٨) الشفقةِ(١١٩) والمَبَرَّة قولُه تعالى: ﴿فَلَعَلَّكَ بَاخِعٌ نَّفْسَكَ عَلَىٰ آثَارِهِمْ إِن لَّمْ يُؤْمِنُوا بِهَٰذَا الْحَدِيثِ أَسَفًا﴾ [الكهف: ٦] أي: قاتلٌ نفْسَكَ لذلك غَضَباً، أو غيظاً، أو جَزَعاً.

ومِثْلُه قولهُ تعالى أيضاً: ﴿لَعَلَّكَ بَاخِعٌ نَّفْسَكَ أَلَّا يَكُونُوا مُؤْمِنِينَ﴾ [الشعراء: ٣] ثم قال: ﴿إِن نَّشَأْ نُنَزِّلْ عَلَيْهِم مِّنَ السَّمَاءِ آيَةً فَظَلَّتْ أَعْنَاقُهُمْ لَهَا خَاضِعِينَ﴾ [الشعراء: ٤]. ومِنْ هذا الباب قولهُ تعالى: ﴿فَاصْدَعْ بِمَا تُؤْمَرُ وَأَعْرِضْ عَنِ الْمُشْرِكِينَ (٩٤) إِنَّا كَفَيْنَاكَ الْمُسْتَهْزِئِينَ (٩٥) الَّذِينَ يَجْعَلُونَ مَعَ اللَّهِ إِلَٰهًا آخَرَ ۚ فَسَوْفَ يَعْلَمُونَ (٩٦) وَلَقَدْ نَعْلَمُ أَنَّكَ يَضِيقُ صَدْرُكَ بِمَا يَقُولُونَ (٩٧)﴾

---

(١١٦) كلمة «واحدة»، لم ترد في المطبوع ولا في نسيم الرياض ولا في شرح القاري.

(١١٧) أسنده المصنف من حديث عبد بن حميد في تفسيره مرسلاً. قال السيوطي في المناهل (٤٤): «ورد ذلك موصولاً عن علي أخرجه ابن مردويه... وأخرج نحوه عن ابن عباس».

(١١٨) نمط: نوع.

(١١٩) في الأصل زيادة: «والرحمة»، ولم ترد في المطبوع، وشرح الخفاجي والقاري.

been ridiculed before you [O Prophet], but those who mocked them were overtaken by what they used to ridicule."[213]

Makkī said that the verses mentioned above were a way of Allah Exalted comforting the Prophet ﷺ and easing the burden he faced from the attacks of the idol worshippers. He informed the Prophet ﷺ that if they continued in their behaviour, they would be punished just like those who came before them. This type of consoling and comforting is also found in the words of Allah Exalted: "If you are rejected by them, so too were Messengers before you."[214] And: "Similarly, no Messenger came to those before them without being told: 'A magician or a madman!'"[215]

Allah Exalted tells the Prophet ﷺ about previous nations and how they slandered their Prophets. He wished to reassure the Prophet ﷺ that he was not the first to face such accusations and that the disbelievers of Makkah resembled those who preceded them. Allah Exalted comforts and excuses the Prophet ﷺ, saying: "So [now] turn away from them [O Prophet]"[216] (meaning, "turn your back and avoid them"), "for you will not be blamed" (i.e., for not successfully communicating the message of Islam to them).[217] There are many verses in which Allah Exalted consoles His Prophet ﷺ in a similar way. To quote a final example, He says: "So be patient with your Lord's decree, for you are truly under Our [watchful] Eyes."[218] Meaning: "Be patient in the face of their attacks, because We are seeing you and protecting you."

---

213 *al-An'ām*, 10.

214 *Fāṭir*, 4.

215 *al-Dhāriyāt*, 52.

216 *al-Dhāriyāt*, 54.

217 *al-Dhāriyāt*, 54.

218 *al-Ṭūr*, 48.

[الحجر: ٩٤ - ٩٧]. وقوله تعالى: ﴿وَلَقَدِ اسْتُهْزِئَ بِرُسُلٍ مِّن قَبْلِكَ فَحَاقَ بِالَّذِينَ سَخِرُوا مِنْهُم مَّا كَانُوا بِهِ يَسْتَهْزِئُونَ﴾ [الأنعام: ١٠]. قال مَكِّيٌّ: سلَّاه الله تعالى[١٢٠] بما ذكر، وهوَّن عليه ما يَلْقَى من المشركين، وأعلمه أنَّ مَنْ تمادَىٰ على ذلك يَحُلُّ به ما حلَّ بمَنْ قَبْله. ومثلُ هذه التسلية قولُه تعالى: ﴿وَإِن يُكَذِّبُوكَ فَقَدْ كُذِّبَتْ رُسُلٌ مِّن قَبْلِكَ﴾ [فاطر: ٤]. ومِنْ هذا قولهُ تعالى: ﴿كَذَٰلِكَ مَا أَتَى الَّذِينَ مِن قَبْلِهِم مِّن رَّسُولٍ إِلَّا قَالُوا سَاحِرٌ أَوْ مَجْنُونٌ﴾ [الذاريات: ٥٢]. عزَّاه الله [تعالى] بما أَخْبَرَه[١٢١] به عن الأمَمِ السالفة ومقالِها لأنبيائهم قَبْله، ومِحْنَتهم بهم؛ وسلَّاه بذلك عن[١٢٢] مِحنَته بمثله من كفَّار مكة، وأنه ليس أوَّلَ مَنْ لقي ذلك، ثم طيَّبَ نفسه، وأبَانَ عُذْرَه بقوله تعالى ﴿فَتَوَلَّ عَنْهُمْ﴾ [الذاريات: ٥٤] أي: أَعْرِض عنهم؛ ﴿فَمَا أَنتَ بِمَلُومٍ﴾ [الذاريات: ٥٤]؛ أي في أداءِ ما بلَّغْتَ وإبلاغِ ما حُمِّلْت. ومثله قوله تعالى: ﴿وَاصْبِرْ لِحُكْمِ رَبِّكَ فَإِنَّكَ بِأَعْيُنِنَا﴾ [الطور: ٤٨] أي: اصْبِرْ على أَذاهم، فإنكَ بحيث نَرَاكَ ونحفظك. سلَّاه الله [تعالى] بهذا في آيٍ كثيرة من هذا المعنى.

(١٢٠) قوله: «الله تعالى»، لم يرد في المطبوع.

(١٢١) في المطبوع: «أخبر».

(١٢٢) في المطبوع: «من».

The Noble Status of Muhammad ﷺ Among the Prophets

Allah Exalted said: "[Remember] when Allah made a covenant with the Prophets, [saying,] 'Now that I have given you the Book and wisdom, if there comes to you a Messenger confirming what you have, you must believe in him and support him.' He added, 'Do you affirm this covenant and accept this commitment?' They said, 'Yes, we do.' Allah said, 'Then bear witness, and I too am a Witness.'"[219]

Abū al-Ḥasan al-Qābisī said: "In this verse, Allah Exalted confirms that He endowed Muhammad ﷺ with certain virtues that He did not give to any other Prophet, and by which he is distinguished." Most scholars of *tafsīr* say that Allah made the "covenant"[220] through Revelation, and that every time He sent a Prophet He would tell them about Muhammad ﷺ, describe him to them, and take a pledge that if they met him they would believe in him. Others said that the pledge was for the Prophets to inform their people and make them promise to inform those who came after them. The phrase "if there comes to you"[221] is addressed to the People of the Book[222] living at the time of the Prophet ﷺ. 'Alī ibn Abī Tālib ﷺ said: "Allah Exalted took a pledge from every Prophet from Adam onwards, that if Muhammad ﷺ was sent whilst they were still alive, they would believe in and support him, and that they would take the same pledge from

219 Āl 'Imrān, 81.

220 ibid.

221 ibid.

222 i.e., Jews and Christians.

الفَصْلُ السَّابع

في ما أَخْبَرَ اللهُ تعالى بِهِ في كتابِهِ العَزِيْزِ مِنْ عَظِيْمِ قَدْرِهِ وشَرِيْفِ مَنْزِلَتِهِ على الأنبياءِ وَحُظْوَةِ رُتْبَتِهِ

قوله تعالى: ﴿وَإِذْ أَخَذَ اللَّهُ مِيثَاقَ النَّبِيِّينَ لَمَا آتَيْتُكُم مِّن كِتَابٍ وَحِكْمَةٍ ثُمَّ جَاءَكُمْ رَسُولٌ مُّصَدِّقٌ لِّمَا مَعَكُمْ لَتُؤْمِنُنَّ بِهِ وَلَتَنصُرُنَّهُ ۚ قَالَ أَأَقْرَرْتُمْ وَأَخَذْتُمْ عَلَىٰ ذَٰلِكُمْ إِصْرِي ۖ قَالُوا أَقْرَرْنَا ۚ قَالَ فَاشْهَدُوا وَأَنَا مَعَكُم مِّنَ الشَّاهِدِينَ﴾ [آل عمران: ٨١].

قال أبو الحسن القابِسي (١٢/ب): استخصَّ الله تعالى محمداً ﷺ بفضْلٍ لم يُؤْتِه غيرَهُ، أَبانَهُ به(١٢٣)، وهو ما ذكره في هذه الآية؛ قال المفسرون: أَخَذَ اللهُ الميثاقَ بالوَحي، فلم يَبْعَثْ نبياً إلا ذكر له محمداً ونَعْتَهُ(١٢٤) وأخذ عليه ميثاقه إنْ أَدْركه ليؤمِنَنَّ به. وقيل: أنْ يُبَيِّنَهُ لقومه، ويأخذَ ميثاقَهم أن يُبَيِّنوه لمَنْ بعدهم. وقوله تعالى: ﴿ثم جاءكم﴾: الخطابُ لأهل الكتاب المعاصرين لمحمد ﷺ.

٣٠- قال عليّ بن أبي طالب رضي اللهُ عنه: لم يبعث الله نبيّاً من آدمَ فمَنْ بَعْده إلا أَخَذَ عليه العَهْدَ في محمد ﷺ، لَئِنْ بُعِثَ - وهو حيٌّ - ليؤمِنَنَّ به

---

(١٢٣) أبانه به: ميّزه به.

(١٢٤) ونَعْتَهُ: وصِفَتَهُ.

their people." Similar was recorded from al-Suddī[223] and Qatādah in reference to other verses. Allah Exalted said: "And [remember] when We took a covenant from the prophets, as well as from you [O Prophet], and from Nūḥ, Ibrāhīm, Mūsā, and 'Īsā ibn Maryam. We did take a solemn covenant from [all of] them"[224]

And: "Indeed, We have sent Revelation to you [O Prophet] as We sent Revelation to Nūḥ and the Prophets after him. We also sent Revelation to Ibrāhīm, Ismā'īl, Isḥāq, Ya'qūb, and his descendants, [as well as] 'Īsā, Ayyūb, Yūnus, Hārūn, and Sulayman. And to Dāwūd We gave the Psalms. There are Messengers whose stories We have told you already and others We have not. And to Mūsā Allah spoke directly. [All were] Messengers delivering good news and warnings so humanity should have no excuse before Allah after [the coming of] the Messengers. And Allah is Almighty, All-Wise. Yet [if you are denied, O Prophet,] Allah bears witness to what He has sent down to you – He has sent it with His Knowledge. The Angels too bear witness. And Allah [alone] is sufficient as a Witness."[225]

It was related that when 'Umar ibn al-Khaṭṭāb ؓ was mourning the death of the Prophet ﷺ, he said: "May my father and mother be your ransom, O Messenger of Allah! As part of your virtue, Allah Exalted sent you as the final Prophet whilst mentioning you among the first, when He said: 'And [remember] when We took a covenant from the prophets, as well as from you [O Prophet], and from Nūḥ, Ibrāhīm, Mūsā, and 'Īsā ibn Maryam. We did take a solemn covenant from [all of] them.'[226] May my father and mother be your ran-

---

223 Ismā'īl ibn 'Abd al-Raḥmān ibn Abī Karīmah, an expert in *tafsīr*. Ibn Ḥajar said: "He was honest, influential, and a fierce opponent of the Shiites." He died in 127 AH. See *Siyar A'lām al-Nubalā'* (5/264).

224 *al-Aḥzāb*, 7.

225 *al-Nisā'*, 163-166.

226 *al-Aḥzāb*, 7.

ولينصُرَنَّه، ويأخذ العَهْدَ بذلك على قومه. ونحوه عن السُّدِّي[١٢٥] وقَتَادَة، في آي تضمنت فَضْلَه من غير وَجْه واحد. قال الله تعالى: ﴿وَإِذْ أَخَذْنَا مِنَ النَّبِيِّينَ مِيثَاقَهُمْ وَمِنكَ وَمِن نُّوحٍ وَإِبْرَاهِيمَ وَمُوسَىٰ وَعِيسَى ابْنِ مَرْيَمَ ۖ وَأَخَذْنَا مِنْهُم مِّيثَاقًا غَلِيظًا﴾ [الأحزاب: ٧].

وقال تعالى: ﴿ إِنَّا أَوْحَيْنَا إِلَيْكَ كَمَا أَوْحَيْنَا إِلَىٰ نُوحٍ وَالنَّبِيِّينَ مِن بَعْدِهِ ۚ وَأَوْحَيْنَا إِلَىٰ إِبْرَاهِيمَ وَإِسْمَاعِيلَ وَإِسْحَاقَ وَيَعْقُوبَ وَالْأَسْبَاطِ وَعِيسَىٰ وَأَيُّوبَ وَيُونُسَ وَهَارُونَ وَسُلَيْمَانَ ۚ وَآتَيْنَا دَاوُودَ زَبُورًا (١٦٣) وَرُسُلًا قَدْ قَصَصْنَاهُمْ عَلَيْكَ مِن قَبْلُ وَرُسُلًا لَّمْ نَقْصُصْهُمْ عَلَيْكَ ۚ وَكَلَّمَ اللَّهُ مُوسَىٰ تَكْلِيمًا (١٦٤) رُّسُلًا مُّبَشِّرِينَ وَمُنذِرِينَ لِئَلَّا يَكُونَ لِلنَّاسِ عَلَى اللَّهِ حُجَّةٌ بَعْدَ الرُّسُلِ ۚ وَكَانَ اللَّهُ عَزِيزًا حَكِيمًا (١٦٥) لَّٰكِنِ اللَّهُ يَشْهَدُ بِمَا أَنزَلَ إِلَيْكَ ۖ أَنزَلَهُ بِعِلْمِهِ ۖ وَالْمَلَائِكَةُ يَشْهَدُونَ ۚ وَكَفَىٰ بِاللَّهِ شَهِيدًا (١٦٦)﴾[١٢٦] [النساء: ١٦٣ - ١٦٦].

٣١- ورُوي عن عمر بن الخطاب رَضِيَ اللهُ عَنْهُ أنه قال في كلام بَكَى[١٢٧] به النبيَّ صَلَّى اللهُ عَلَيْهِ وَسَلَّمَ، فقال: بأبي أنتَ وأُمي، يا رسول الله! لقد بلغ من فَضِيلتك عند الله أَنْ بعثك آخِرَ الأنبياء، وذَكَرك في أولهم، فقال: : ﴿وَإِذْ أَخَذْنَا

---

(١٢٥) هو إسماعيل بن عبد الرحمن بن أبي كريمة، إمام مفسر، قال ابن حجر: «صدوق يَهِمُ، ورمي بالتشيع» مات سنة (١٢٧ هـ). انظر ترجمته في سير أعلام النبلاء ٥/٢٦٤.

(١٢٦) في الأصل: «وكيلاً»، وأثبت الناسخ فوقها: «التلاوة: شهيداً». قلت: هو الصحيح.

(١٢٧) بكى: أي رَثَىٰ. وفي المطبوع: «زَكَّى» بدل «بكىٰ».

som, O Messenger of Allah! As part of your virtue, even the people of the Hellfire will wish that they followed you when they are being punished in its depths, and they will say: 'Oh! If only we had obeyed Allah and obeyed the Messenger!'[227]"[228]

Qatādah related: "The Prophet ﷺ said: 'I was the first Prophet to be created and the last to be sent.'"[229] Because of that, he is mentioned in the verses above before Nūḥ ﷺ. Al-Samarqandī said: "Our Prophet ﷺ is elevated by being mentioned before the other Prophets, even though he was the last to be sent. The meaning is that Allah Exalted took a covenant from them when they were dispersed from the seed of Adam like tiny specks."

Allah Exalted said: "We have chosen some of those messengers above others. Allah spoke directly to some, and raised some high in rank. To 'Īsā ibn Maryam, We gave clear proofs and supported him with the holy spirit. If Allah had willed, succeeding generations would not have fought [among themselves] after receiving the clear proofs. But they differed..."[230]

The scholars of *tafsīr* say that "...and raised some high in rank"[231] refers to Muhammad ﷺ, because he was sent to the Red and the Black (i.e., all of humanity), the spoils of war were made permissible for him, he was able to perform miracles, and there was no gift be-

227 *al-Aḥzāb*, 66.

228 Suyūṭī said in *Al-Manāhil*, p. 47: "I did not find this narration."

229 Reported by Ibn Sa'd in *Al-Ṭabaqāt* in a *mursal* narration from Qatādah, and Ibn Rajab in *Majālis fī al-Sīrat al-Nabī* ﷺ, p. 23, where he commented: "It was reported by Ṭabarānī from the chain of Qatādah, from al-Ḥasan, from Abū Hurayrah, in a *marfū'* narration, and the *mursal* narration resembles it." Also reported from the hadith of Abū Hurayrah by Ibn Abī Ḥātim in his *Tafsīr*, Ibn Lāl in *Makārim al-Akhlāq*, and Abū Nu'aym in *Al-Dalā'il*. Al-Ḥawt said in *Asnā al-Muṭālib*, p. 170: "The chain contains Baqiyyah ibn al-Walīd, who used to practice *tadlīs* (i.e., the concealing of defects or weaknesses in the chain), and Sa'īd ibn Bashīr, who was a weak narrator." See also *Al-Maqāṣid al-Ḥasanah* (837), *Mawārid al-Ẓam'ān* (2093), and *Fayḍ al-Qadīr* (5/53).

230 *al-Baqarah*, 253.

231 *al-Baqarah*, 253.

مِنَ النَّبِيِّينَ مِيثَاقَهُمْ وَمِنكَ وَمِن نُّوحٍ وَإِبْرَاهِيمَ وَمُوسَىٰ وَعِيسَى ابْنِ مَرْيَمَ ۖ وَأَخَذْنَا مِنْهُم مِّيثَاقًا غَلِيظًا﴾ [الأحزاب: ٧]. بأبي أنتَ وأمّي يا رسول اللهِ! لقد بلغ من فضيلتك عنده أنَّ أهل النار يودُّون أن يكونوا أطاعُوكَ وهم بينَ أَطْباقها يعذَّبون يقولون: ﴿يَا لَيْتَنَا أَطَعْنَا اللَّهَ وَأَطَعْنَا الرَّسُولَا﴾(١٢٨) [الأحزاب: ٦٦].

٣٢- قال قَتَادة: إنَّ النبيَّ ﷺ قال: «**كنتُ أوَّلَ الأنبياءِ في الخَلْق، وآخرَهم في البَعْثِ**»(١٢٩)، فلذلك وقع ذِكْرُه مقدما هنا قبل نوح وغيره.

قال السَّمَرْقَنْدِي: في هذا تفضيلُ نبينا - عليه السلام - لتخصيصه في الذِّكر(١٣٠) قَبْلَهم، وهو آخرُهم. المعنى: أخذ اللهُ [تعالى] عليه الميثاق، إذ أخرجهم من ظَهْرِ آدم كالذَّرّ. وقال تعالى: ﴿۞ تِلْكَ الرُّسُلُ فَضَّلْنَا بَعْضَهُمْ عَلَىٰ بَعْضٍ ۘ مِّنْهُم مَّن كَلَّمَ اللَّهُ ۖ وَرَفَعَ بَعْضَهُمْ دَرَجَاتٍ ۚ وَآتَيْنَا عِيسَى ابْنَ مَرْيَمَ الْبَيِّنَاتِ وَأَيَّدْنَاهُ بِرُوحِ الْقُدُسِ ۗ وَلَوْ شَاءَ اللَّهُ مَا اقْتَتَلَ الَّذِينَ مِن بَعْدِهِم مِّن بَعْدِ مَا جَاءَتْهُمُ الْبَيِّنَاتُ وَلَٰكِنِ اخْتَلَفُوا﴾ [البقرة: ٢٥٣].

---

(١٢٨) قال السيوطي في مناهل الصفا (٤٧): «لم أجده».

(١٢٩) أخرجه من حديث قتادة مرسلاً: ابنُ سعد في الطبقات، وأورده الحافظ ابن رجب في مجالس في سيرة النبي صلى الله عليه وسلم ص (٢٣) وقال «خرجه الطبراني من رواية قتادة، عن الحسن، عن أبي هريرة مرفوعاً والمرسلُ أشبهُ». وخرجه أيضاً من حديث أبي هريرة: ابنُ أبي حاتم في التفسير، وابن لال في مكارم الأخلاق، وأبو نعيم في الدلائل. قال الحوت في أسنى المطالب ص (١٧٠): «فيه بقية بن الوليد مدلّسٌ، وسعيد بن بشير ضعيف». وسيأتي برقم (٦٣٧). وانظر المقاصد الحسنة (٨٣٧)، وموارد الظمآن (٢٠٩٣)، وفيض القدير ٥/٥٣.

(١٣٠) في المطبوع: «بالذكر».

stowed upon any other Prophet except he was given the same. Some commentators added that whereas Allah Exalted addresses the other Prophets by their names, He only addresses Muhammad ﷺ by reference to his Prophethood and Messengership, saying "O Prophet!"[232] or "O Messenger!"[233]

Al-Samarqandī related that al-Kalbī said, in his commentary of the verse "And indeed, one of those who followed his way was Ibrāhīm"[234], that the pronoun "his" refers to Muhammad ﷺ. Meaning: "Ibrāhīm ﷺ is from those who followed the way of Muhammad ﷺ"; i.e., in religion and methodology. Al-Farrā' allowed this interpretation and Makkī related it from him. Others said that it refers to Nūḥ ﷺ.

232 e.g., *al-Taḥrīm*, 1.

233 e.g., *al-Mā'idah*, 41.

234 *al-Ṣaffāt*, 83.

قال أهلُ التفسير: أراد بقوله: ﴿وَرَفَعَ بَعْضَهُمْ دَرَجَاتٍ ۚ﴾ [البقرة: ٢٥٣]. محمداً ﷺ؛ لأَنه بُعِث إلى الأحمر والأسود، وأُحِلَّت له الغنائمُ، وظهرت على يديه المعجزاتُ، وليس أحدٌ من الأنبياء أُعطي فضيلةً أو كرامةً إلا وقد أُعطِي محمدٌ ﷺ مِثْلَها. قال بعضهم: ومن فضله أنَّ اللّٰهَ تعالى خاطب الأنبياءَ بأسمائهم، وخاطبه بالنبوَّة والرسالةِ في كتابه، فقال: ﴿يا أَيها النَّبِيُّ﴾ و ﴿يا أيُّها الرَّسُولُ﴾. وحكى السَّمَرْقَنديُّ عن الكَلْبي - في قوله تعالى: ﴿۞ وَإِنَّ مِن شِيعَتِهِ لَإِبْرَاهِيمَ﴾ [الصافات: ٨٣] - أن الهاءَ عائدةٌ على محمد؛ أي إنَّ من شِيعَةِ محمد لإبراهيم؛ أي على دينه ومِنْهَاجه. وأجازه الفرَّاء، وحكاه عنه مَكّيٌّ. وقيل: المرادُ منه نوح عليه السلام.

Allah Exalted Instructing His Creation to Send Prayers Upon the Prophet ﷺ, His Protection of the Prophet ﷺ, & His Removal of Punishment Because of Him

Allah Exalted said: "But Allah would never punish them while you [O Prophet] were in their midst."[235] This referred to the people of Makkah. When the Prophet ﷺ had left the city and some believers remained, Allah revealed: "Nor would He ever punish them if they prayed for forgiveness."[236]

Similarly, Allah Exalted says "Had those [unknown] believers stood apart, We would have certainly inflicted a painful punishment on the disbelievers."[237] And: "[We would have let you march through Makkah,] had there not been believing men and women, unknown to you. You might have trampled them underfoot, incurring guilt for [what you did to] them unknowingly. That was so Allah may admit into His Mercy whoever He wills."[238]

However, when the believers migrated from Makkah, He said: "And why should Allah not punish them".[239] This sequence of revelation is one of the clearest confirmations of the honoured status of the Prophet ﷺ. Allah Exalted diverted punishment from the people of Makkah because of his presence, and then because of the presence of his Companions after him. When they had all left, He punished

---

235 *al-Anfāl*, 33.

236 *al-Anfāl*, 33.

237 *al-Fatḥ*, 25.

238 *al-Fatḥ*, 25.

239 *al-Anfāl*, 34.

الفَصْلُ الثامِن

فِيْ إعْلامِ اللهِ تعالى خَلْقَه بِصَلاتِهِ عَلَيْهِ وولايَتِهِ لَهُ ورَفْعِهِ العَذابَ بِسَبَبِهِ

قال الله تعالى: ﴿وَمَا كَانَ اللَّهُ لِيُعَذِّبَهُمْ وَأَنتَ فِيهِمْ﴾ [الأنفال: ٣٣]؛ أي: ما كُنْتَ بمكة. فلما خرج النبيُّ ﷺ من مكة، وبَقِيَ فيها مَنْ بقي من المؤمنين نزل: ﴿وَمَا كَانَ اللَّهُ مُعَذِّبَهُمْ وَهُمْ يَسْتَغْفِرُونَ﴾ [الأنفال: ٣٣]. وهذا مِثْلُ قوله: ﴿لَوْ تَزَيَّلُوا لَعَذَّبْنَا الَّذِينَ كَفَرُوا مِنْهُمْ عَذَابًا أَلِيمًا﴾ [الفتح: ٢٥].

وقوله [تعالى]: ﴿وَلَوْلَا رِجَالٌ مُّؤْمِنُونَ وَنِسَاءٌ مُّؤْمِنَاتٌ لَّمْ تَعْلَمُوهُمْ أَن تَطَئُوهُمْ فَتُصِيبَكُم مِّنْهُم مَّعَرَّةٌ بِغَيْرِ عِلْمٍ لِّيُدْخِلَ اللَّهُ فِي رَحْمَتِهِ مَن يَشَاءُ﴾ [الفتح: ٢٥]. فلما هاجر المؤمنون نزلت: ﴿وَمَا لَهُمْ أَلَّا يُعَذِّبَهُمُ اللَّهُ﴾ [الأنفال: ٣٤]. وهذا من أَبْيَنِ ما يُظْهِرُ مكانته ﷺ.

وَدَرَأَ به(١٣١) العذابَ عن أهل مكة بسبب كَوْنِه، ثم كَوْنِ أصحابه بعده بين أَظْهُرِهم، فلما خلَتْ مكةُ منهم عذَّبهم [اللهُ] بتسليطِ المؤمنين عليهم، وغَلبتهم إياهم، وحَكَّمَ فيهم سيوفَهم، وأورثهم أَرْضَهم وديارهم وأموالَهم.

وفي الآية أيضاً تأويلٌ آخر.

---

(١٣١) في نسخة: «وَدَرْأَتُهُ»، أي: دَفْعُهُ.

those who remained by granting the believers victory over them. They took control of the city and inherited the land, homes, and wealth of its inhabitants. Other interpretations of the verses have also been recorded.

I read the following hadith to the esteemed scholar Abū ʿAlī ﷺ, who said: "It was narrated from Abū Faḍl ibn Khayrūn and Abū al-Ḥusayn al-Ṣayrafī, who both said: 'It was narrated from Abū Yaʿlā (better known as Ibn Zawj al-Ḥurrah), from Abū ʿAlī al-Sinjī, from Muhammad ibn Maḥbūb al-Marwazī, from Abū ʿĪsā al-Ḥāfiẓ[240], from Sufyān ibn Wakīʿ, from Ibn Numayr, from Ismāʿīl ibn Ibrāhīm ibn Muhājir, from ʿAbbād ibn Yūsuf, from Abū Burdah ibn Abī Mūsā, from his father[241], who said: "The Messenger of Allah ﷺ said: 'Allah revealed to me two reassurances for my nation: "But Allah would never punish them while you [O Prophet] were in their midst. Nor would He ever punish them if they prayed for forgiveness."[242] So, when I pass away, I leave seeking forgiveness with them.'"'"[243]

In the same vein, Allah Exalted said: "We have sent you [O Prophet] only as a mercy for the whole world."[244] The Messenger of Allah ﷺ also said: "I am a source of safety and security to my Companions."[245] Some scholars interpreted his words to mean safety "from innovations", "from differing", or "from trials". Others observed: "The Messenger of Allah ﷺ was the greatest source of safety and

---

240 Better known as Tirmidhī.

241 Abū Mūsā al-Ashʿarī.

242 *al-Anfāl*, 33.

243 The author reports the narration from the chain of Tirmidhī in his *Sunan* (3082). Tirmidhī said: "This hadith is *gharīb*, and Ismāʿīl ibn Muhājir is weak." Suyūṭī graded the hadith as *ḍaʿīf* in *Al-Jāmiʿ al-Ṣaghīr* (2722). It was related by Ibn Abī Ḥātim in a *marfūʿ* narration from Ibn ʿAbbās, and by Abū al-Shaykh in a *marfūʿ* narration from Abū Hurayrah.

244 *al-Anbiyā'*, 107.

245 Reported by Muslim (2531) from the hadith of Abū Mūsā al-Ashʿarī, with the wording: "I am source of safety and security to my Companions."

٣٣- حدثنا القاضي الشهيد أبو علي - رحمه الله - بقراءتي عليه، [قال]: حدثنا أبو الفضل بن خَيْرون، وأبو الحُسين الصَّيْرفي، قالا: حدثنا أبو يَعْلى ابن زَوْج الحُرَّة، حدثنا أبو علي السِّنْجِي، حدثنا محمد بن محبوب المَرْوَزي، حدثنا أبو عيسى الحافظ، حدثنا سفيان بن وَكيع، حدثنا ابن نُمَير، عن إسماعيل بن إبراهيم بن مُهاجر، عن عبّاد بن يوسف، عن أبي بُرْدَةَ بن أبي موسى، عن أبيه؛ قال: (٣١/أ) قال رسول الله ﷺ: «أنزلَ اللهُ عليَّ أمانَيْنِ لأُمتي: ﴿وَمَا كَانَ اللَّهُ لِيُعَذِّبَهُمْ وَأَنتَ فِيهِمْ ۚ وَمَا كَانَ اللَّهُ مُعَذِّبَهُمْ وَهُمْ يَسْتَغْفِرُونَ﴾ [الأنفال: ٣٣] فإذا مضيت تركتُ فيهم الاستغفار»[١٣٢]. ونحوٌ منه قوله تعالى: ﴿وَمَا أَرْسَلْنَاكَ إِلَّا رَحْمَةً لِّلْعَالَمِينَ﴾ [الأنبياء ١٠٧].

٣٤- [و] قال عليه السلام: «أَنا أمانٌ لأَصحابي»[١٣٣]. قيل: من البِدَع.

و قيل: من الإختلاف و الفِتَن. قال بعضُهم: الرسولُ ﷺ هو الأمانُ الأعظم ما عاشَ، و ما دامت سُنَّتُه باقيةً فهو باقٍ، فإذا أُميتَت سنَّتهُ فانتظِروا البلاءَ و الفِتَن. و قال الله تعالى: ﴿إِنَّ اللَّهَ وَمَلَائِكَتَهُ يُصَلُّونَ عَلَى النَّبِيِّ ۚ يَا أَيُّهَا الَّذِينَ آمَنُوا صَلُّوا عَلَيْهِ وَسَلِّمُوا تَسْلِيمًا﴾

---

(١٣٢) أسنده المصنف من طريق أبي عيسىٰ الترمذي في سننه (٣٠٨٢) وقال: «حديث غريب وإسماعيل بن مهاجر يضعف الحديث». ورمز لضعفه السيوطي في الجامع الصغير (٢٧٢٢) ورواه أبن أبي حاتم عن ابن عباس موقوفاً، وأبو الشيخ عن أبي هريرة موقوفا نحوه.

(١٣٣) أخرجه مسلم (٢٥٣١) من حديث أبي موسى الأشعري بلفظ «أنا أمنةٌ لأصحابي»، وسيورده المصنف بهذا اللفظ برقم (٦٤٩).

security whilst he was alive, and as long as his Sunnah remains he is present. If his Sunnah dies out, then beware of trials and hardship."

Allah Exalted said: "Indeed, Allah showers His Blessings upon the Prophet, and His Angels pray for him. O believers! Invoke Allah's Blessings upon him, and salute him with worthy greetings of peace."[246] Allah confirms the virtue of His Prophet ﷺ by sending His Blessings upon him, then the blessings of the Angels, and then commanding His servants to send their prayers and salutations. Abū Bakr ibn Fūrak[247] reported that some scholars referred to this verse in interpreting the saying of the Prophet ﷺ: "The prayer was made the coolness of my eyes[248]."[249] They understood the narration as: "The Prophet ﷺ found tranquillity in the Blessings of Allah Exalted, the prayers of the Angels, and His Command for His servants to send the same, until the Day of Judgement." The verse uses the word "*ṣalāh*" in all three cases: from Allah b it refers to His Mercy, but from the Angels and us it refers to supplication. Others interpreted "*ṣalāh*" as "blessings". However, when the Prophet ﷺ taught others how to send prayers upon him, he made a distinction between "*ṣalāh*" and "blessings". We will return to the subject of sending prayers upon the Prophet ﷺ later in the text.

Some scholars mentioned, in their commentary of "*Kāf Hā Yā 'Ayn Ṣād*"[250], that the "*Kāf*" refers to "*kifāyah*", or "sufficiency", as in "the sufficiency of Allah Exalted for His Prophet ﷺ". As Allah Exalt-

---

246 *al-Aḥzāb*, 56.

247 Muhammad ibn al-Ḥasan ibn Fūrak, a righteous scholar, and leading figure in the field of dialectics. He died in 406 AH. See *Siyar A'lām al-Nubalā'* (17/214).

248 i.e., a source of peace and tranquility.

249 Reported by Nasā'ī (7/61), Aḥmad (3/128), Abū Ya'lā (3482), Bayhaqī (7/87), and others, from the hadith of Anas ibn Mālik. Authenticated by Ḥākim (2/160), and Dhahabī agreed. 'Irāqī approved of the chain. Ibn Ḥajar graded the hadith as *ḥasan*, and Suyūṭī shared the same view.

250 *Maryam*, 1.

[الأحزاب: ٥٦]. أبانَ[١٣٤] اللهُ تعالىٰ فَضْلَ نبيّه صلى الله عليه و سلم بصلاته عليه، ثم بصلاةِملائكتهِ، وَ أَمَرَ عباده بالصلاة و التسليم عليه.

٣٥- [وقد حكى أبوبكر بن فُوْرَك[١٣٥] أن بعضَ العلماء تأوّل قولَه ﵇: «وجُعِلتْ قُرَّةُ عَيْنِي في الصلاة»[١٣٦] على هذا؛ أي في صلاةِ الله تعالى عليّ و ملائكتهِ وأَمْرِهِ الأُمةَ بذلك إلى يوم القيامة] والصلاةُ من الملائكة ومنّا له دعاءٌ، ومن الله [عزَّ و جلَّ] رحمةٌ.

وقيل : يُصَلُّون: يُبَارِكون. وقد فرَّقَ النبيُّ ﷺ - حين علَّم الصلاةَ عليه - بين لفظِ الصلاة و البركة.

وسنذكر حكم الصلاة عليه. وذكر بعضُ المتكلمين في تفسير حروف ﴿كهيعص﴾ [مريم: ١] أن الكافَ من (كافٍ)، أي كفاية الله [تعالى] لنبيه، قال [تعالى]: ﴿أَلَيْسَ اللَّهُ بِكَافٍ عَبْدَهُۥ﴾ [الزمر: ٣٦]. والهاء: هدايته [له]، قال: ﴿وَيَهْدِيَكَ صِرَاطًا مُّسْتَقِيمًا﴾ [الفتح: ٢]. والياء: تأييده له، قال: ﴿هُوَ الَّذِى أَيَّدَكَ بِنَصْرِهِ وَبِالْمُؤْمِنِينَ﴾ [الأنفال: ٦٢]. والعين: عِصْمَتهُ له قال: ﴿وَاللَّهُ يَعْصِمُكَ مِنَ النَّاسِ﴾

---

(١٣٤) أبان: أظهر.

(١٣٥) هو الإمام، العلامة، الصالح، شيخ المتكلمين: محمد بن الحسن بن فُوْرَك. توفي سنة (٤٠٦ هـ). انظر ترجمته في سير أعلام النبلاء ٢١٤/١٧.

(١٣٦) أخرجه النسائي ٦١/٧، وأحمد ١٢٨/٣، وأبو يعلى (٣٤٨٢)، والبيهقي ٨٧/٧ وغيره من حديث أنس بن مالك، وصححه الحاكم ١٦٠/٢ وأقره الذهبي، وجوَّد إسناده الحافظ العراقي، وحسنه ابن حجر، وتبعه السيوطي. وسيعيده المصنف برقم (١٤٥، ١٤٦، ٣٠٢).

ed revealed: "Is Allah not sufficient for His servant?"[251] The "*Hā*" was said to refer to His "*hidāyah*", or "guidance" for the Prophet ﷺ. As Allah Exalted said: "[so that Allah may] guide you along the Straight Path".[252] The "*Yā*" was said to refer to His "*ta'yīd*", or "support" for the Prophet ﷺ. Allah Exalted said: "He is the One Who has supported you with His Help".[253] The "'Ayn" was understood as His "*'iṣmah*", or "preservation" of the Prophet ﷺ. As Allah Exalted affirms: "Allah will [certainly] protect you from the people."[254] And the "*Ṣād*" was interpreted as His "*ṣalāh*", or "prayers" upon the Prophet ﷺ. As Allah Exalted says: "Indeed, Allah showers His Blessings upon the Prophet, and His Angels pray for him."[255] Allah Exalted revealed: "But if you [continue to] collaborate against him, then [know that] Allah Himself is his Guardian. And Jibrīl, the righteous believers, and the Angels are [all] his supporters as well."[256] "His Guardian" means "his Protector". "The righteous believers" has been variously understood as "the Prophets"; "the Angels"; "Abū Bakr ؓ and 'Umar ؓ"; "'Alī ؓ"; or simply "the believers", in accordance with its most apparent meaning.

---

251 *al-Zumar*, 36.

252 *al-Fatḥ*, 2.

253 *al-Anfāl*, 62.

254 *al-Mā'idah*, 67.

255 *al-Aḥzāb*, 56.

256 *al-Taḥrīm*, 4.

[المائدة: ٦٧]. و الصاد: صلاته عليه؛ قال: ﴿إِنَّ اللَّهَ وَمَلَٰٓئِكَتَهُۥ يُصَلُّونَ عَلَى النَّبِيِّ ﴾ [الأحزاب: ٥٦] وقال تعالى: ﴿وَإِن تَظَٰهَرَا عَلَيْهِ فَإِنَّ اللَّهَ هُوَ مَوْلَىٰهُ وَجِبْرِيلُ وَصَٰلِحُ الْمُؤْمِنِينَ ۖ وَالْمَلَٰٓئِكَةُ بَعْدَ ذَٰلِكَ ظَهِيرٌ﴾ [التحريم: ٤] ﴿مولاه﴾ أي: وليّه. ﴿وصالحُ المؤمنين﴾ قيل: الأنبياء. وقيل: الملائكة. وقيل : أبو بكر، وعُمر. وقيل: عليّ. وقيل : المؤمنون على ظاهِره.

The Honour Bestowed Upon The Prophet ﷺ in Surah Al-Fath

Allah Exalted said: "Indeed, We have granted you a clear triumph [O Prophet] so that Allah may forgive you for your past and future shortcomings, perfect His Favour upon you, guide you along the Straight Path, and so that Allah will help you tremendously. He is the One Who sent down serenity upon the hearts of the believers so that they may increase even more in their faith. To Allah [alone] belong the forces of the heavens and the earth. And Allah is All-Knowing, All-Wise. So He may admit believing men and women into Gardens under which rivers flow – to stay there forever – and absolve them of their sins. And that is a supreme achievement in the sight of Allah. Also [so that] He may punish hypocrite men and women and polytheistic men and women, who harbour evil thoughts of Allah. May ill-fate befall them! Allah is displeased with them. He has condemned them and prepared for them Hell. What an evil destination! To Allah [alone] belong the forces of the heavens and the earth. And Allah is Almighty, All-Wise. Indeed, [O Prophet,] We have sent you as a witness, a deliverer of good news, and a warner, so that you [believers] may have faith in Allah and His Messenger, support and honour him, and glorify Allah morning and evening. Surely those who pledge allegiance to you [O Prophet] are actually pledging allegiance to Allah. Allah's Hand is over theirs. Whoever breaks their pledge, it will only be to their own loss. And whoever fulfils their pledge to Allah, He will grant them a great reward."[257]

In these verses, Allah Exalted elucidates His Bounties upon and

---

257 *al-Fatḥ*, 1-10.

الفَصلُ التاسع

فِيْ ما تَضَمَّنَتْهُ سُورَةُ الفَتحِ مِنْ كَراماتِهِ ﷺ

قال تعالى: ﴿إِنَّا فَتَحْنَا لَكَ فَتْحًا مُّبِينًا (١) لِّيَغْفِرَ لَكَ اللَّهُ مَا تَقَدَّمَ مِن ذَنبِكَ وَمَا تَأَخَّرَ وَيُتِمَّ نِعْمَتَهُ عَلَيْكَ وَيَهْدِيَكَ صِرَاطًا مُّسْتَقِيمًا (٢) وَيَنصُرَكَ اللَّهُ نَصْرًا عَزِيزًا (٣) هُوَ الَّذِى أَنزَلَ السَّكِينَةَ فِى قُلُوبِ الْمُؤْمِنِينَ لِيَزْدَادُوا إِيمَانًا مَّعَ إِيمَانِهِمْ ۗ وَلِلَّهِ جُنُودُ السَّمَاوَاتِ وَالْأَرْضِ ۚ وَكَانَ اللَّهُ عَلِيمًا حَكِيمًا (٤) لِّيُدْخِلَ الْمُؤْمِنِينَ وَالْمُؤْمِنَاتِ جَنَّاتٍ تَجْرِى مِن تَحْتِهَا الْأَنْهَارُ خَالِدِينَ فِيهَا وَيُكَفِّرَ عَنْهُمْ سَيِّئَاتِهِمْ ۚ وَكَانَ ذَٰلِكَ عِندَ اللَّهِ فَوْزًا عَظِيمًا (٥) وَيُعَذِّبَ الْمُنَافِقِينَ وَالْمُنَافِقَاتِ وَالْمُشْرِكِينَ وَالْمُشْرِكَاتِ الظَّانِّينَ بِاللَّهِ ظَنَّ السَّوْءِ ۚ عَلَيْهِمْ دَائِرَةُ السَّوْءِ ۖ وَغَضِبَ اللَّهُ عَلَيْهِمْ وَلَعَنَهُمْ وَأَعَدَّ لَهُمْ جَهَنَّمَ ۖ وَسَاءَتْ مَصِيرًا (٦) وَلِلَّهِ جُنُودُ السَّمَاوَاتِ وَالْأَرْضِ ۚ وَكَانَ اللَّهُ عَزِيزًا حَكِيمًا (٧) إِنَّا أَرْسَلْنَاكَ شَاهِدًا وَمُبَشِّرًا وَنَذِيرًا (٨) لِّتُؤْمِنُوا بِاللَّهِ وَرَسُولِهِ وَتُعَزِّرُوهُ وَتُوَقِّرُوهُ وَتُسَبِّحُوهُ بُكْرَةً وَأَصِيلًا (٩) إِنَّ الَّذِينَ يُبَايِعُونَكَ إِنَّمَا يُبَايِعُونَ اللَّهَ يَدُ اللَّهِ فَوْقَ أَيْدِيهِمْ ۚ فَمَن نَّكَثَ فَإِنَّمَا يَنكُثُ عَلَىٰ نَفْسِهِ ۖ وَمَنْ أَوْفَىٰ بِمَا عَاهَدَ عَلَيْهُ اللَّهَ فَسَيُؤْتِيهِ أَجْرًا عَظِيمًا (١٠)﴾ [الفتح: ١ - ١٠].

تضمّنت هذه الآيات من فضله والثناء عليه، وكريم منزلته عند الله تعالىٰ،

Praise for the Prophet ﷺ, who is blessed with an honoured station with His Lord. He begins by confirming His Decree for the Prophet ﷺ to overcome his enemies, and for His Law to reign supreme. He informs the Prophet ﷺ that he has been forgiven, and will not be taken to task for actions of the past or future. Some scholars said that "forgiveness" here refers both to things that have occurred and things that have not. Makkī commented: "Allah Exalted made His Favour a cause of His Forgiveness. Everything is from Him, and there is no deity worthy of worship except Allah. Favour upon Favour, and Bounty upon Bounty."

Then, Allah Exalted said: "So that Allah may...perfect His favour upon you"[258]. Some scholars said: "By causing those who had previously shown arrogance towards the Prophet ﷺ to submit." Others interpreted the verse to refer to the conquests of Makkah and Ṭā'if. And another opinion states: "By elevating the renown of the Prophet ﷺ in this world, aiding him, and forgiving him." All these positions can be reconciled. Allah Exalted is informing His Prophet ﷺ that to "perfect His Favour"[259] includes subduing his arrogant enemies, conquering the land most important and beloved to him[260], elevating his renown, guiding him to the Straight Path (the Path which leads to Paradise and complete happiness), and aiding him with a great victory. He shows His Favour to the believers by filling their hearts with peace and tranquillity, informing them of impending triumph and forgiveness from their Lord, and covering their mistakes; and by destroying their enemies in this life and the Hereafter, cursing them, distancing them from His Mercy, and promising them a terrible fate.

Then, Allah Exalted says: "Indeed, [O Prophet,] We have sent you

---

258 *al-Fatḥ*, 2.

259 ibid.

260 i.e., Makkah.

ونِعْمَتِه لديه، ما يَقْصُر الوصْفُ عن الإنتهاءِ إليه؛ فابتدأ - جلَّ جلالهُ - بإعلامه بما قَضَاهُ له من القضاءِ البَيِّن بظهوره، وغلبته على عدوه (١٤/أ) وعُلوِّ كلمتهِ وشريعته، و أَنه مغفورٌ له، غير مؤاخذٍ بما كان و ما يكون.

قال بعضُهم: أراد غُفْران ما وقع و ما لم يَقَعْ، أي إنك مغفور لك.

وقال مَكِّيٌّ: جعل [اللهُ] المِنَّةَ سبباً للمغفرة، و كلٌّ مِنْ عنده، لا إله غيره، [١٨] مِنَّةً بعد مِنَّةٍ، و فضلاً بعد فَضْل.

ثم قال : ﴿وَيُتِمَّ نِعْمَتَهُ عَلَيْكَ﴾ [الفتح: ٢] قيل: بخضوع مَنْ تكبّر عليك(١٣٧).

وقيل: بفَتْح مكةَ والطائف.

وقيل: يرْفَع ذِكْرك في الدنيا و ينصرك و يغفر لك؛ فأَعلمه بتمام نعمته عليه بخضوع متكبري عدوِّه له، وفَتْح أهمِّ البلاد عليه و أحبها له، ورَفْع ذكره، و هدايتهِ الصراطَ المستقيم المبلِّغ الجنةَ و السعادةَ، ونَصْرِه النصرَ العزيز، ومِنَّته على أُمته المؤمنين بالسكينة و الطمأنينة التي جعلها في قلوبهم، وبِشَارَتِهم بما لَهُمْ بَعْدُ، وفَوْزِهم العظيم، والعَفْوِ عنهم، والسترِ لذنوبهم، وهلاَكِ عدوِّه في الدنيا والآخرةِ، ولَعْنِهم وبُعْدِهم من رحمته، وسوء مُنْقَلبهم.

ثم قال: ﴿إِنَّا أَرْسَلْنَاكَ شَاهِدًا وَمُبَشِّرًا وَنَذِيرًا (٨) لِّتُؤْمِنُوا بِاللَّهِ وَرَسُولِهِ وَتُعَزِّرُوهُ وَتُوَقِّرُوهُ وَتُسَبِّحُوهُ بُكْرَةً وَأَصِيلًا﴾ [الفتح: ٨،

(١٣٧) في الأصل «تكبر لك»، والمثبت من المطبوع.

as a witness, a deliverer of good news, and a warner, so that you [believers] may have faith in Allah and His Messenger, support and honour him, and glorify Allah morning and evening."[261] Here, He illustrates some special qualities and characteristics of the Prophet ﷺ; namely, his position as a witness over his community and a Messenger to them. In interpreting this verse, some scholars commented that the Prophet ﷺ bears witness to his nation about the Oneness of Allah. He delivers good news regarding their reward, or their forgiveness. And he warns his enemies of impending punishment. Others said that he warns them to forsake misguidance, so that whoever was predestined to do so will believe in Allah. To "support... him"[262] was said to mean "to celebrate him", "to come to his aid", or "to emphasize his prestige". And to "honour him"[263] was interpreted as: "to hold him in high regard". A non-canonical[264] Qur'anic recitation reads the word "*tu'azzirūhū*", translated here as "[to] support... him"[265], as "*tu'azzizū*hū", with a *zā*, meaning "to glorify". The majority opinion states that both terms refer to Muhammad ﷺ. Then, the verse says "and glorify [Him]", which refers back to Allah Exalted.

Ibn 'Aṭā' said: "A number of blessings upon the Prophet ﷺ are combined in this surah: 'a clear triumph'[266], which is a sign of being answered; forgiveness[267], which is a sign of His Love; the perfection of His Favour[268], which is a sign of his special status with Allah; and guidance[269], which is a sign of His Protection. 'Forgiveness' im-

261 *al-Fatḥ*, 8-9.

262 *al-Fatḥ*, 9.

263 ibid.

264 "*Shādh*".

265 *al-Fatḥ*, 9.

266 *al-Fatḥ*, 1.

267 Refers to *al-Fatḥ*, 2.

268 ibid.

269 ibid.

٩] فَعَدَّ^(۱۳۸) محاسنه وخصائصه، مِن شهادتِه على أُمته لنفسه، بِتَبْلِيغِهِ الرسالةَ لهم.

وقيل: شاهِداً لهم بالتوحيد، ومُبَشِّراً لأُمَّتِهِ بالثواب. وقيل: بالمغفرة. ومُنْذِراً عدوَّه بالعذاب.

وقيل: مُحَذِّراً مِن الضلالات لِيُؤمن بالله، ثم به [ﷺ] مَنْ سبقت له مِن الله الحُسْنى. ويُعَزِّرُوه؛ أي يُجِلُّونه. وقيل: ينصرونه.

وقيل: يبالغون في تَعْظيمه. ويُوَقِّرُوهُ؛ أَيْ يعظموهُ^(۱۳۹).

وقرأ بعضُهم: ﴿تُعَزِّزُوه﴾^(١٤٠) بزايين: مِن العِزِّ، والأكثر والأظهر أنَّ هذا في حقّ محمد ﷺ.

ثم قال: ﴿وتُسَبِّحوه﴾؛ فهذا راجعٌ إلى الله تعالى.

قال ابنُ عطاء: جُمع للنبي ﷺ في هذه السورة نِعَمٌ مختلفةٌ، مِن الفَتْحِ المُبين، وهو مِن أعلامِ الإجابة، والمَغْفِرة، وهي مِن أعلامِ المحبَّة، وتمامِ النعمة، وهي مِن أعلامِ الإختصاصِ، والهداية، وهي مِن أعلامِ الولاية، فالمغفرةُ تبرئةٌ مِن العيوب، وتمامُ النعمةِ: إبلاغُ الدرجةِ الكاملة، والهدايةُ: (١٤/ب) وهي الدعوةُ إلى المشاهدة.

---

(۱۳۸) في الأصل «فعدَّدَ»، والمثبت من المطبوع.

(۱۳۹) في الأصل «يعظمونه»، والمثبت من المطبوع.

(١٤٠) وهي قراءة شاذة.

plies absolution from faults, receiving 'the perfection of His Favour' means reaching the degree of perfection, and 'guidance' is the call to bear witness." Ja'far ibn Muhammad said: "As part of the perfection of His Favour, He made the Prophet ﷺ His Beloved, swore upon his life, abrogated previous laws through him, raised him to the highest station, protected him during the miraculous Night Journey so that his 'sight never wandered, nor did it overreach'[270], sent him to all of humanity, made the spoils of war permissible for him, granted him the ability to intercede for others, elevated him as the leader of the children of Adam, joined the mention of Allah with the mention of His Prophet ﷺ and His Pleasure with his, and made the Prophet ﷺ one of the two pillars of belief[271]."

The surah continues: "Surely those who pledge allegiance to you [O Prophet] are actually pledging allegiance to Allah. Allah's Hand is over theirs."[272] This verse refers to the Pledge of Riḍwān[273]. "The Hand of Allah" was said to mean: "the Power of Allah", "the reward of Allah", "the Favour of Allah", or "the covenant of Allah". In a similar way, Allah Exalted says: "It was not you [believers] who killed them, but it was Allah Who did so. Nor was it you [O Prophet] who threw [a handful of sand at the disbelievers], but it was Allah Who did so".[274] Whereas the first example is metaphorical the second is literal, because no human being would have had the ability to throw it in such a way that every single person among the enemy's ranks had their eyes filled with sand. In reality, it was Allah Exalted who created the action of throwing and gave the Prophet ﷺ the ability to achieve this feat. The fighting of the Angels was likewise a literal

---

270 *al-Najm*, 17.

271 "*Tawḥīd*".

272 *al-Fatḥ*, 10.

273 "The Pledge of Pleasure", also known as "the Pledge of the Tree".

274 *al-Anfāl*, 17.

وقال جعفر بن محمد: من تمام نعمته عليه أنْ جعله حَبِيبَه، وأقسم بحياته، ونَسَخَ به شرائعَ غيره، وعَرَج به إلى المَحلّ الأعلى، وحفِظَه في المعراج حتى ما زاغَ البَصَرُ وما طَغَى، وبعثه إلى الأسود والأحمر، وأحل له ولأمته الغنائمَ، وجعله شَفِيعاً مُشفَّعاً، وسيِّدَ وَلدِ آدم، وقَرَن ذِكْرَه بذكره، ورِضاهُ برضاهُ، وجعله أحدَ رُكْنَي التوحيد.

ثم قال تعالى: ﴿إِنَّ الَّذِينَ يُبَايِعُونَكَ إِنَّمَا يُبَايِعُونَ اللَّهَ يَدُ اللَّهِ فَوْقَ أَيْدِيهِمْ ۚ﴾ يعني: بيعة الرضوان؛ أي إنما يبايعونَ اللهَ بِبَيْعَتِهِمْ إياكَ.

﴿يَدُ اللَّهِ فَوْقَ أَيْدِيهِمْ ۚ﴾ يريد: عند البَيْعَة. قيل: قوة الله، وقيل: ثَوَابه. وقيل: مِنَّته. وقيل: عَقْده، وهذه استعارةٌ، وتجنيس في الكلام، وتأكيد لعَقْد بَيْعتهم إياه. وعِظَم شَأْنِ المُبايَع ﷺ.

وقد يكون مِنْ هذا قولُه تعالى: ﴿فَلَمْ تَقْتُلُوهُمْ وَلَٰكِنَّ اللَّهَ قَتَلَهُمْ ۚ وَمَا رَمَيْتَ إِذْ رَمَيْتَ وَلَٰكِنَّ اللَّهَ رَمَىٰ ۚ﴾ [الأنفال: ١٧]؛ وإنْ كان الأول في باب المجاز، وهذا في باب الحقيقة، لأنَّ القاتل والرامي بالحقيقة هو اللهُ، وهو خالقُ فِعْله وَرَمْيِهِ، وقُدْرَتِه عليه ومسبِّبُه، ولأنه ليس في قدرة البشر توصيلُ تلك الرَّميةِ حيثُ وصلَتْ، حتى لم يَبْقَ منهم مَنْ لم تملأ عَيْنَيه، وكذلك قَتْلُ الملائكة لهم حقيقة.

وقد قيل في هذه الآية الأخرىٰ:

إنها على المجاز العربي، ومقابلةِ اللفظ ومناسبتهِ؛ أي: ما قتلتموهم، وما رَمَيْتَهمْ أَنتَ إذ رميت وجوهَهم بالحَصْباء والتراب، ولكنّ اللهَ رمى قلوبَهم

rather than metaphorical event. Others proposed that the latter verse is based on an Arabic saying, and gave the meaning as: "It was not you that threw stones and dust in their faces. Rather, Allah Exalted struck (or 'threw') fear into their hearts."

بالجزَع، أي إنَّ منفعةَ الرَّمْي كانت من فِعْلِ اللهِ؛ فهو القاتلُ والرامي
بالمعنى وأنتَ بالاسم.

Other Examples of Allah Exalted Elucidating the Honoured Status of the Prophet ﷺ

One example of Allah Exalted demonstrating the lofty station of the Prophet ﷺ is the miraculous Night Journey, which is described in Surahs al-Isrā' and al-Najm. Similarly, his position is confirmed by the protection offered by His Lord, who says: "Allah will [certainly] protect you from the people."[275] "And [remember, O Prophet,] when the disbelievers conspired to capture, kill, or exile you. They planned, but Allah also planned. And Allah is the best of planners."[276]

And: "[It does not matter] if you [believers] do not support him, for Allah did in fact support him when the disbelievers drove him out [of Makkah] and he was only one of two. While they both were in the cave, he reassured his companion, 'Do not worry; Allah is certainly with us.' So Allah sent down His Serenity upon the Prophet, supported him with forces you [believers] did not see, and made the word of the disbelievers lowest, while the Word of Allah is supreme. And Allah is Almighty, All-Wise."[277] In this event, Allah Exalted averted the harm of the enemies of the Prophet ﷺ who had secretly plotted to kill him. When the Prophet ﷺ went out to them, Allah Exalted made them blind to his presence, and later He caused them not to look for him in the cave[278]. These signs, the tranquillity which fell upon the Prophet ﷺ and Abū Bakr ؓ, and the story of Surāqah

---

275 *al-Mā'idah*, 67.

276 *al-Anfāl*, 30.

277 *al-Tawbah*, 40.

278 In which he was hiding with Abū Bakr ؓ.

الفَصْل العَاشر

فِيْ مَا أَظْهَرَهُ اللهُ تَعالى فِي كِتَابِهِ العَزِيْزِ مِنْ كَرامَتِهِ عَلَيْهِ وَمَكَانَتِهِ عِنْدَهُ وما خصَّهُ [اللّه] بِهِ مِنْ ذلكَ سِوَى ما انْتَظَمَ فيما ذكرناهُ قَبْلُ

من ذلك ما نَصَّهُ(١٤١) تعالى من(١٤٢) قصة الإسراء في سورة: ﴿سبحان﴾ و ﴿النَّجم﴾ وما انطوت عليه القصةُ من عظيم منزلته وقُربه (١٥/أ) ومشاهدته ما شاهَدَ من العجائب.

ومن ذلك عِصْمتهُ من الناس بقوله [تعالى]: ﴿وَاللَّهُ يَعْصِمُكَ مِنَ النَّاسِ﴾ [المائدة: ٦٤]. وقوله [تعالى]: ﴿وَإِذْ يَمْكُرُ بِكَ الَّذِينَ كَفَرُوا لِيُثْبِتُوكَ أَوْ يَقْتُلُوكَ أَوْ يُخْرِجُوكَ ۚ وَيَمْكُرُونَ وَيَمْكُرُ اللَّهُ ۖ وَاللَّهُ خَيْرُ الْمَاكِرِينَ﴾ [الأنفال: ٣٠].

وقوله: ﴿إِلَّا تَنصُرُوهُ فَقَدْ نَصَرَهُ اللَّهُ إِذْ أَخْرَجَهُ الَّذِينَ كَفَرُوا ثَانِيَ اثْنَيْنِ إِذْ هُمَا فِي الْغَارِ إِذْ يَقُولُ لِصَاحِبِهِ لَا تَحْزَنْ إِنَّ اللَّهَ مَعَنَا ۖ فَأَنزَلَ اللَّهُ سَكِينَتَهُ عَلَيْهِ وَأَيَّدَهُ بِجُنُودٍ لَّمْ تَرَوْهَا وَجَعَلَ كَلِمَةَ الَّذِينَ كَفَرُوا السُّفْلَىٰ ۗ وَكَلِمَةُ اللَّهِ هِيَ الْعُلْيَا ۗ وَاللَّهُ عَزِيزٌ حَكِيمٌ﴾ [التوبة: ٤٠]. وما دفع(١٤٣) اللّهُ به عنه في هذه القصة من أذاهم بعد

---

(١٤١) في المطبوع: «قصّه».

(١٤٢) في المطبوع: «في».

(١٤٣) في المطبوع: «رفع».

ibn Mālik[279], are all highlighted by scholars of hadith and Sīrah[280] in connection to the story of the cave[281] and the hadith concerning the migration of the Prophet ﷺ[282].

Allah Exalted also informs the Prophet ﷺ of His Blessings upon him in Surah al-Kawthar: "Indeed, We have granted you [O Prophet] abundant goodness. So pray and sacrifice to your Lord [alone]. Only the one who hates you is truly cut off [from any goodness]."[283] "*Al-Kawthar*", translated here as "abundant goodness"[284], has also been interpreted as "His Pond", "a river in Paradise", "[the ability of] intercession", "[the ability to perform] numerous miracles", "Prophethood", and "deep understanding". At the end of the surah, Allah Exalted responds to the enemies of the Prophet ﷺ, saying: "Only the one who hates you is truly cut off [from any goodness]."[285] "*Shāni'aka*", translated here as "the one who hates you"[286], also means "your enemy", and "the one who…is truly cut off"[287] is "a miserable, despicable person", "a person who is totally alone", or "a person with no good in him whatsoever."

Allah Exalted says: "We have certainly granted you the seven oft-repeated verses and the great Qur'an."[288] The "seven oft-repeat-

---

279 Reported by Bukhārī (3908) and Muslim (2009/91) from the hadith of al-Barā' ibn 'Āzib. Also reported by Bukhārī (3906) from Surāqah himself, and again (3911) from the hadith of Anas ibn Mālik.

280 The study of the life of the Prophet ﷺ.

281 Reported by Bukhārī (3922) and Muslim (2381), from the hadith of Abū Bakr ؓ.

282 Reported by Bukhārī (3905) from the hadith of 'Ā'ishah, and again (3911) from the hadith of Anas. Also reported by Muslim (2009) from the hadith of al-Barā' ibn 'Āzib.

283 *al-Kawthar*, 1-3.

284 *al-Kawthar*, 1.

285 *al-Kawthar*, 3.

286 ibid.

287 ibid.

288 *al-Ḥijr*, 87.

تحزُّبهم لهُلْكه وخلوصِهم نَجِيّاً في أمره، والأخذِ على أبصارهم عند خروجه عليهم، و ذهولِهِم عن طلبه في الغار، وما ظهر في ذلك من الآيات، و نزول السكينة عليه.

٣٦- وَقِصَّةِ سُرَاقَةَ بن مالك[١٤٤]، حسبَ ماذكره أهلُ الحديث والسِّير.

٣٧- في قصة الغار[١٤٥].

٣٨- وحديث الهجرة[١٤٦].

ومنه قوله تعالى: ﴿إِنَّا أَعْطَيْنَاكَ الْكَوْثَرَ (١) فَصَلِّ لِرَبِّكَ وَانْحَرْ (٢) إِنَّ شَانِئَكَ هُوَ الْأَبْتَرُ (٣)﴾ [الكوثر: ١ - ٣].

أعلمه اللهُ عَزَّوَجَلَّ بما أعطاه. و ﴿الكوثَرُ﴾: حَوْضُه. وقيل: نهر في الجنة. وقيل: الخير الكثير. وقيل: الشفاعة. وقيل: المعجزات الكثيرة. وقيل: النبوة. وقيل: المعرفة.

ثم أَجابَ عنه عدوَّه، وردّ عليه قوله، فقال [تعالى]: ﴿إِنَّ شَانِئَكَ هُوَ الْأَبْتَرُ﴾؛ أي عدُوَّك ومُبْغِضَكَ. و﴿الأبتر﴾: الحقير الذليل، أو المفرد الوحيد، أو الذي لا خير فيه.

---

(١٤٤) قصة سراقة رواها البخاري (٣٩٠٨)، ومسلم (٩١/٢٠٠٩) من حديث البراء بن عازب، والبخاري (٣٩٠٦) من حديث سراقة نفسه. و(٣٩١١) من حديث أنس بن مالك.

(١٤٥) قصة الغار رواها البخاري (٣٩٢٢)، ومسلم (٢٣٨١) من حديث أبي بكر الصديق.

(١٤٦) حديث الهجرة رواه البخاري (٣٩٠٥) من حديث عائشة، و(٣٩١١) من حديث أنس، ورواه مسلم (٢٠٠٩) من حديث البراء بن عازب

ed"[289] were said to refer to the seven lengthy surahs at the beginning of the Qur'an, with "the great Qur'an"[290] indicating Surah al-Fātiḥah. Others understood the phrase "seven oft-repeated"[291] to refer to Surah al-Fātiḥah on its own, and "the great Qur'an"[292] to mean the rest of the Book. Another opinion suggests "seven oft-repeated"[293] refers to seven aspects of the Qur'an; namely, "commands, prohibitions, glad tidings, warnings, parables, enumeration of His Blessings, and news of the great Qur'an itself."

Some scholars said that Surah al-Fātiḥah was named "the seven oft-repeated verses"[294] because it is recited in every unit (*raka'ah*) of prayer. Others observed that Allah Exalted specifically saved His Qur'an for Muhammad ﷺ out of all His Prophets, as a permanent store [of guidance] for him. The Qur'an was also said to be called "the seven oft-repeated"[295] because of the stories repeated within it. Another interpretation understood the phrase to refer to seven Blessings Allah Exalted bestowed upon His Prophet ﷺ: guidance, Prophethood, mercy, intercession, protection, honour, and tranquillity.

Allah Exalted said: "And We have sent down to you [O Prophet] the Reminder, so that you may explain to people what has been revealed for them, and perhaps they will reflect."[296] "We have sent you [O Prophet] only as a deliverer of good news and a warner to all of humanity."[297]

---

289 ibid.

290 ibid.

291 ibid.

292 ibid.

293 ibid.

294 ibid.

295 ibid.

296 *al-Naḥl*, 44.

297 *Saba'*, 28.

وقال تعالى: ﴿وَلَقَدْ آتَيْنَاكَ سَبْعًا مِّنَ الْمَثَانِي وَالْقُرْآنَ الْعَظِيمَ﴾ [الحِجْر: ٨٧].

قيل: السبع المَثَاني: السُّورُ الطِّوالُ الأُوَلُ. ﴿والقرآن العظيم﴾: أم القرآن. وقيل: السبع المثاني: أمُّ القرآن. والقرآن العظيم: سائره. وقيل: السبع المثاني: ما في القرآن، من أَمْر، ونهى، وبُشْرى، وإنذار، وضَرْب مثَل، وإعداد نِعَم، وآتيناك نبأَ القرآن العظيم.

وقيل: سميت أُمُّ القرآن مَثَاني لأنها تُثَنَّي في كل ركعة[١٤٧]. وقيل: بل اللهُ [تعالى] استثناها لمحمد ﷺ، وادخَرها[١٤٨] له دون سائرِ[١٤٩] الأنبياء.

وسُمّي القرآنُ مثاني: لأن القِصَصَ تثنَّي فيه.

وقيل: السبع المثاني: أكرمناك بِسَبْع كرامات: الهدي، والنبوة، والرحمة، والشفاعة، والولاية، والتعظيم، والسكينة.

وقال: ﴿وَأَنزَلْنَا إِلَيْكَ الذِّكْرَ لِتُبَيِّنَ لِلنَّاسِ مَا نُزِّلَ إِلَيْهِمْ وَلَعَلَّهُمْ يَتَفَكَّرُونَ﴾ [النحل: ٤٤].

وقال: ﴿وَمَا أَرْسَلْنَاكَ إِلَّا كَافَّةً لِّلنَّاسِ بَشِيرًا وَنَذِيرًا﴾ [سبأ: ٢٨].

وقال تعالى: ﴿قُلْ يَا أَيُّهَا النَّاسُ إِنِّي رَسُولُ اللَّهِ إِلَيْكُمْ جَمِيعًا

---

(١٤٧) أي تكرر في كل صلاة.

(١٤٨) في المطبوع: «وذخرها». أي جعلها ذخيرة.

(١٤٩) كلمة: «سائر»، لم ترد في المطبوع.

Again, Allah Exalted enumerates the special characteristics of the Prophet ﷺ: "Say, [O Prophet,] 'O humanity! I am Allah's Messenger to you all. To Him [alone] belongs the kingdom of the heavens and the earth. There is no god [worthy of worship] except Him. He gives life and causes death.' So believe in Allah and His Messenger, the unlettered Prophet, who believes in Allah and His Revelations. And follow him, so you may be [rightly] guided."[298]

Allah Exalted said: "We have not sent a Messenger except in the language of his people to clarify [the message] for them."[299] The previous Prophets were each sent to a specific community, whereas Muhammad ﷺ was sent to all creation. As the Messenger of Allah ﷺ himself said: "I was sent to the red and the black."[300]

Allah Exalted said: "The Prophet has a stronger affinity to the believers than they do themselves. And his wives are their mothers."[301] The scholars of *tafsīr* said: "a stronger affinity to the believers than they do themselves"[302] means: "His instructions to them follow the example of a master instructing his servants." Others understood the verse to imply: "Following his instructions is more befitting than following their own opinions." "And his wives are their mothers"[303] refers to the fact that it was impermissible for anyone to marry the wives of the Prophet ﷺ after his death. This was a special dispensation for the Prophet ﷺ, and they will also be his wives in the Hereafter. There was a non-canonical recitation of the verse which included

---

298 *al-Aʿrāf*, 158.

299 *Ibrāhīm*, 4.

300 Reported by Ṭabarānī in *Al-Awsaṭ* from Abū Saʿīd al-Khudrī. Haythamī graded the chain as *ḥasan* in *Majmaʿ al-Zawāʾid* (8/269). Reported by Muslim (521) from Jābir, with the wording: "I was sent to every red and black person [i.e., all of humanity]." The hadith is originally taken from Bukhārī (335).

301 *al-Aḥzāb*, 6.

302 ibid.

303 ibid.

الَّذِى لَهُ مُلْكُ السَّمَاوَاتِ وَالْأَرْضِ ۖ لَا إِلَٰهَ إِلَّا هُوَ يُحْيِي وَيُمِيتُ ۖ فَآمِنُوا بِاللَّهِ وَرَسُولِهِ النَّبِيِّ الْأُمِّيِّ الَّذِى يُؤْمِنُ بِاللَّهِ وَكَلِمَاتِهِ وَاتَّبِعُوهُ لَعَلَّكُمْ تَهْتَدُونَ﴾ [الأعراف: ١٥٨] قال الفقيه القاضي - رحمه الله - : فهذه (١٥/ب) من خصائصه.

وقال تعالى: ﴿وَمَا أَرْسَلْنَا مِن رَّسُولٍ إِلَّا بِلِسَانِ قَوْمِهِ لِيُبَيِّنَ لَهُمْ ۖ﴾ [إبراهيم: ٤] فخصَّهم بقومهم، وبعث محمداً صلى الله عليه و سلم إلى الخَلْق كافَّة.

٣٩- كما قال عليه السلام: «بُعِثْتُ إلى الأَحْمَرِ والأَسْوَدِ»(١٥٠).

وقال تعالى: ﴿النَّبِيُّ أَوْلَىٰ بِالْمُؤْمِنِينَ مِنْ أَنفُسِهِمْ ۖ وَأَزْوَاجُهُ أُمَّهَاتُهُمْ ۗ﴾ [الأحزاب: ٦].

قال أهل التفسير: ﴿أَوْلَىٰ بِالْمُؤْمِنِينَ مِنْ أَنفُسِهِمْ ۖ﴾ أي: ما أنفذه فيهم من أمر فهو ماضٍ عليهم كما يَمْضي حكم السيد على عبده.

وقيل: اتباع أمره أَوْلى من اتباع رَأْي النَّفْس.

﴿وَأَزْوَاجُهُ أُمَّهَاتُهُمْ ۗ﴾ أي: هنَّ في الحرمة(١٥١) كالأمهات؛ حرَّمَ نكاحهنَّ عليهم بَعْدَهُ؛ تَكْرِمة له وخُصوصية، ولأنهن له أزواجٌ في الآخرة.

---

(١٥٠) رواه الطبراني في الأوسط من حديث أبي سعيد الخدري. قال الحافظ الهيثمي في مجمع الزوائد ٢٦٩/٨: «إسناده حسن». وأخرجه مسلم (٥٢١) من حديث جابر بلفظ: «وبعثت إلى كل أحمر وأسود». وأصل الحديث في البخاري (٣٣٥). وأراد بالأحمر والأسود: جميع العالم.

(١٥١) (الحرمة): الاحترام والتعظيم.

the phrase "and he [i.e., the Prophet ﷺ] is their father", but it is no longer extant due to its divergence from the universally-accepted text of the Qur'an[304].[305]

Allah Exalted said: "Allah has revealed to you the Book and wisdom and taught you what you never knew. Great [indeed] is Allah's favour upon you!"[306] The "Great...favour"[307] of Allah was interpreted as "Prophethood", or "the reward awaiting him in Eternal Paradise". Al-Wāsiṭī said that it indicates his ability to bear the vision [of his Lord] that Mūsā ﷺ could not bear.

HERE ENDS THIS SELECTION FROM "THE SHIFA".

---

304 i.e., the *muṣḥaf* of ʿUthmān.

305 Al-Khafājī and others said it is a *shādh* recitation. Suyūṭī said in *Al-Manāhil*, p. 52: "It was reported by Ibn Rāhawayh in his *Musnad* from Ubayy ibn Kaʿb." The author has discounted the recitation, as you see in the text.

306 *al-Nisā'*, 113.

307 ibid.

٤٠- وقد قرىء: وهو أبٌ لهم(١٥٢). ولا يُقْرأ به الآن لمخالفته المصحف.

وقال [الله] تعالى: ﴿وَأَنزَلَ اللَّهُ عَلَيْكَ الْكِتَابَ وَالْحِكْمَةَ وَعَلَّمَكَ مَا لَمْ تَكُن تَعْلَمُ ۚ وَكَانَ فَضْلُ اللَّهِ عَلَيْكَ عَظِيمًا﴾ [النساء: ١١٣].

قيل: فَضْلُه العظيم بالنبوة. وقيل: بما سبق له في الأزل. وأشار الواسطيّ إلى أنها إشارةٌ إلى احتمال الرؤية التي لم يحتملْها موسىٰ، صلىٰ الله عليهما.

(١٥٢) في المناهل (٥٢): «أخرجها ابن راهويه في مسنده عن أُبَيّ بن كعب». وقد ردّها القاضي عياض كما ترى. وهي قراءة شاذة كما قال الخفاجي وغيره.

Printed in Poland
by Amazon Fulfillment
Poland Sp. z o.o., Wrocław

32369298R00072